CHAPTER ONE
Introduction   1

CHAPTER TWO
Physical Abuse   23

CHAPTER THREE
Neglect: Physical, Medical, Educational   45

CHAPTER FOUR
Emotional and Verbal Abuse   73

CHAPTER FIVE
Sexual Abuse   103

CHAPTER SIX
Contemporary Social Issues   129

FOREWORD

I first met Dr. Venessa Brown years ago when she was a social worker for the DeKalb County, Georgia, Department of Children and Family Services and I was a DeKalb County Juvenile Court judge presiding over cases concerning abused, neglected, and deprived children. At that time, her dedication to the best interests of the children and her insight into their circumstances impressed me, and I considered the children with whom she worked to be fortunate, indeed, to have her as an advocate. I have followed her career with interest as she broadened her horizons into academia, applying her practical knowledge to teaching. It is with pride that I introduce this book of case studies, which will allow her to reach beyond the confines of the classroom to educate many more students. By reading and analyzing actual case studies, answering questions, and critiquing these cases, students will learn to synthesize basic theory with reality, bridging the gap between "learning" and "doing." This book will be invaluable in helping students to develop skills that they will ultimately use to serve the best interests of real children in desperate circumstances, helping those children to rise above abuse, neglect, and deprivation with the goal of becoming productive citizens.

Senior Judge Edward D. Wheeler
Decatur, Georgia

PREFACE

Case studies are very valuable in child welfare practice as well as social work practice. They are a part of social work history and were used to set the stage for what we now know as social work practice. The documentation of the Mary Ellen case in 1874 set the stage for child welfare practice, and is a case that is widely used to discuss early child welfare history.

It is exciting to see case studies in child welfare become a vital part of social work education today. Students tend to learn better by actually working with cases from the field. Using cases as an introduction to child welfare practice is valuable because students and new practitioners get firsthand experience working with children and families, and they are not disillusioned about the complexities of this field of practice. The use of case studies will continue to be applicable as we strive to understand the complexity of problems that plague children and families.

Case studies in child welfare are valuable across disciplines as families present with multiple issues (e.g., biological, psychological, social). Case studies help to link theoretical frameworks from other disciplines to what is practical in working with children and families. Case vignettes and case scenarios as well as full case studies are already being included in social work and other human services fields texts to help guide students in their understanding of content and concepts.

PLAN FOR THE TEXT

The book is designed to provide students and practitioners with actual case studies from the field of child welfare. The chapters are arranged so that the reader gets a sense of diverse cases in child welfare practice, including questions to guide a student through safety and risk assessments, a family case analysis, and an opportunity to become familiar with assessment diagrams. Also, at the end of each chapter is a brief list of suggested readings for further understanding of working with children and families. Chapter 1 is an overview of child abuse and neglect and also gives an understanding of how to do a case analysis. Chapter 2 includes cases that have issues of physical abuse. Students will have an opportunity to see how physical abuse is manifested in different families. Chapter 3 consists of cases that deal with various forms of neglect. Poverty and neglect of children are among the most horrible forms of maltreatment. Chapter 4 consists of cases that include issues of emotional and verbal abuse. These cases are often difficult to assess, but this is an opportunity to expose students to this type of maltreatment. Chapter 5 consists of cases that deal with the sexual abuse of children. Child sexual abuse cases are emotional but are a reality in our society. They are probably the most difficult to deal with, because students are forced to deal with their own values, ethics, and biases when it comes to working with the alleged perpetrator. Overall, students will have an opportunity to address their biases from a systems theoretical perspective and recognize the value of treating the whole family. The book concludes with Chapter 6, which consists of cases that deal directly with some of the most prevalent contemporary societal problems. Although all of the cases deal with societal problems, these cases pay particular attention to specific problems and might present more complex analysis.

A MESSAGE TO THE STUDENT

Many of you who use these cases will be new to the profession of social work and the field of child welfare. You have embarked on one of the most exciting fields of practice in social work practice and education today. The case studies in this book will give you an overview of the kinds of complex problems and issues facing children and families in the child welfare profession. The cases will help guide you through child welfare practice and the family case assessment process.

The cases will give meaning to helping you integrate theory with practice. You will be challenged to look at the cases from a systems perspective. All too often, workers in child welfare assess only the issues surrounding the child and not those of the family. You will see the value of treating the whole family system. The cases will help you understand why the generalist perspective and the strengths perspective are so valuable in working with children and families. You will struggle with your value system, encountering ethical dilemmas that will challenge you. This is good. The questions and assessment diagrams at the end of each chapter will direct your analysis and assist you in processing the complexities and diversity of issues embedded in each case. The questions will guide you through a case analysis. Performing case analyses will strengthen your problem-solving skills and help you to assess a family situation better.

For many of you, working with people might not be a new adventure, but working in child welfare might be. Webb (1996) states: "Social workers in child welfare settings have a multifaceted role—one that includes direct work with culturally diverse children and families; work with the family court and the department of social services; and the necessity of functioning on an inter-disciplinary team" (p. 223). I hope that these actual cases will benefit you and give you an introduction to the diverse kinds of problems, cultural values, social and economic justice, poverty, safety, and risk factors facing children and families in the twenty-first century.

I hope this book will help you understand the value of doing a case analysis and allow you to process a case through the generalist problem-solving method. You will process the case by exploring the family and learning to engage, assess, plan, design a case plan, and finally use two assessment diagrams (ecomaps and genograms) to help guide you in un-derstanding the dynamics of the family. Webb (1996) notes that "it is impor-tant for social workers in this field of practice to have a solid knowledge base in child assessment, including diagnostic classifications, family sys-tems assessment, substance abuse assessment, and evaluation of the impact of trauma on children (especially that resulting from physical and sexual abuse)" (p. 223). The cases will expose you to different diverse cultures, challenge your practice skills, and help you understand families who come from different socioeconomic backgrounds.

A MESSAGE TO THE INSTRUCTOR

First, let me take this opportunity to thank you for choosing *Child Welfare: Case Studies*. I know that you will find this book a very useful tool in creating a classroom of learning that is exciting and stimulating. You will find that these cases will encourage students to think critically about the assessments they make when working with children and families. Case method learning can help you create class conditions conducive to active learning and can initiate an empowering and active experience for learners. It has been sug-gested that this method of learning encourages "student-generated" analy-sis rather than teacher-manufactured analysis (Rivas & Hull, 1996).

The complexity of these cases will help to create a classroom climate that is stimulating, empowering, challenging, and exciting to students as they strive to integrate theory and practice. These cases will help students incorporate knowledge from their previous courses: social work practice, child welfare, and human behavior.

I hope that students will find these cases challenging and useful in guiding them in their work with children and families. I also think it is an opportunity for students to try out the interpersonal skills that they have learned by role-playing the cases in a classroom setting. The cases are diverse enough that students will have the opportunity to confront some of their biases and, most of all, challenge some of their cultural beliefs and work toward cultural competency as families redefine themselves in the twenty-first century.

I hope that students will enjoy working with actual cases from the field. The field of child welfare is very complex, and families today present with multiple problems. Many of them will treasure the hands-on experience that these cases will bring to their educational preparation for the field of child welfare.

Writing this book was an opportunity for me to share my experience from my work in child welfare. I have had many valuable experiences in the field, and my ten years in the trenches have cemented my commitment to working on behalf of children and families in our society. My clients were my best teachers. They taught me the value of meeting them right where they were and also the value of working from a strengths perspective regardless of how bad their situations were. Carl Rogers says it best when he says that clients ultimately know the solutions to their own problems. I often remind students that our job as social work practitioners is to empower our clients and support them as they begin to work through their pain and their often traumatic life experiences. The analogy that I often use in class is that people's lives are often like a ball of yarn and that our job is to help them peel away the layers of pain and weave in all of their strengths and resources, and ultimately to work with them until they are able to manage their own lives.

Thank you for choosing *Child Welfare: Case Studies* and for finding my years in the trenches a value worth sharing. I hope you find these cases as rewarding and beneficial in your teaching of working with children and families as I have.

ABOUT THE AUTHOR

Venessa Ann Brown, M.S.W., Ph.D., is an assistant professor of social work at Southern Illinois University at Edwardsville (SIUE). Dr. Brown has written articles about her child welfare experiences and has trained child welfare workers in clinical practice. She authored *From One Hand to Another: The Story of a Sexually Abused Child's Strength and Courage*, published by Reflections.

Dr. Brown brings to the writing of this book more than ten years of experience in child welfare practice. She has worked as a protective services investigator for the DeKalb County Department of Children and Family Services in DeKalb County, Georgia. Her career has included teaching at Greenville College and at Southern Illinois University—Edwardsville.

In addition to her teaching, she has traveled to South Africa looking at child welfare issues from a global perspective. She hopes to continue her research in international child welfare issues in South Africa, the Caribbean, and Central and South America.

ACKNOWLEDGMENTS

This book represents my work with children and families during my ten years as a social worker in child welfare. All of the case materials have been disguised to protect client confidentiality. The social work profession and the field of child welfare owe a debt to children and families for allowing us to become effective practitioners by using their stories to educate future social workers and human services professionals regardless of their field of study. Thank you to my clients who told me their stories and enriched my life.

I cannot possibly name all of the significant people and influences in my life who contributed indirectly to this book. You know who you are, and I thank you. However, I must thank those who have contributed new knowledge to enhancing the child welfare profession, and the family theorists who, recognizing that children cannot function without their families, saw the need to create a body of knowledge that included the entire family system. Many thanks to my friends at the DeKalb County Department of Children and Family Services for all of your support over the years and for always remembering me as a part of the family. I miss you all.

My colleagues at Southern Illinois University—Edwardsville, Dr. Kathleen Tunney and Dr. Monica White, deserve special recognition for reading my manuscript and giving me many helpful suggestions for improving it. Also, thanks to Dr. Judy Cingaloni and colleagues for their early contributions to the writing of this book. Thank you for valuing my work. I am indebted to my secretaries, Judy Zimmerman and Karen York, who typed, edited, and supported me throughout the writing of this book. Thank you for your kindness. I can never forget Rudy Wilson, assistant provost for social and cultural diversity at SIUE, for believing in me and providing some summer support so I could work on my book. Many thanks to Dr. Roslyn Sykes, who has informally mentored me during our travels to South Africa. Special thanks to Dr. Richard Lyle and Dr. Robert Waymer at Clark Atlanta University School of Social Work, who have always encouraged me and believed in me.

Special thanks to Enrique Howell, my graduate student, who supported me with all of the complicated tasks and assisted me with all of my graphic designs. Thank you for your commitment to ensuring that children and families are respected and protected. It has been a delight to see you develop professionally in the field of child welfare over the past few years. In addition, thank you to all of my students who engaged in the many discussions about child welfare and family case analysis. More than anything, thank you for allowing me to share with you my years in the trenches to enhance your academic experience.

A number of people provided me with support and counsel as I developed my ideas for writing this book. Some good friends who encouraged me and anchored me during my many storms are Dr. Abdul Turay, Dr. Bill Woods, and Dr. Marvin Finkleston (my mentors), Barbara Johnson, Jennifer Hamer, Virginia Baker, Albert Seline, Sharon and Maurice Almon, Karen McGill, Fredrick Thompson, and Mom and Dad Hollister. To my lifelong student and friend, Cathy Burgos, thank you for your support and for providing a place of refuge when I needed solitude. To my cruise partner Cynthia Jackson, who was with me when I first discovered cruising as a "way of living" that has ultimately changed my life. Special thanks to all my friends at sea and across the world, especially Carlos Quea, who created a climate where I could think and write, and most of all for enhancing my life and stretching my world view.

I owe special thanks to Judy Fifer and Alyssa Pratt at Allyn and Bacon for taking an interest in my work, and ensuring that the voices of my children and families are heard. Also, thank you to the following reviewers for their comments on the manuscript: Joan Abbey, University of Michigan; Carol Boyd, Delta State University; George W. Caulton, Western New England College; Mary Collins, Boston University; John Herrick, Michigan State University; John Kayser, University of Denver; and Carol Massat, University of Illinois–Chicago. Also, thank you to Erica Graff at Allyn and Bacon for encouraging me to submit a prospectus.

Finally, my deepest appreciation is to God and my parents, Richard and Clytee Brown. Thanks for your prayers. Special thanks to my family, Everett Harrington, Velma, Cynthia, Richard Jr. (Junebug), Wayne, and Britney. They tolerated me when I was frustrated, supported me, listened to the many stories, and cheered me along the way. Without question I owe a debt to my little brother George, who is my confidante and friend. Thank you for all the kind words and flowers, and for celebrating all of my victories. Congratulations on your new business, "Heroes At Home" barber shop. Special thanks to all of your barbers, clients, and friends who have encouraged me along the way.

REFERENCES

Rivas, R. F., & Hull, G., Jr. (1996). *Case Studies in Generalist Practice*. Pacific Grove, CA: Brooks/Cole.

Webb, N. B. (1996). *Social Work Practice with Children*. New York: The Guilford Press.

CHAPTER ONE

INTRODUCTION

Children are very important to our society, and they are our future. They have hopes and dreams, and they need our protection. The field of child welfare can no longer assess the well-being of children alone. Child welfare professionals must assess the child within the context of their family. Webb (1996) states: "Children and their families are interdependent. Therefore, when one member of a family system experiences difficulties, the stress reverberates to all members of the family. Although a child may be singled out as having a 'problem,' the practitioner must look beyond the individual and think about the meaning and significance of that problem to all the family members, in order to understand the problem's source and to determine how best to focus helping efforts" (p. 115). Child welfare is becoming more complex as families are plagued with more social ills. Families no longer seek counseling for one problem; they have many. More than ever, issues surrounding children require that the child be assessed within his or her own environment, because the family is the most dominant part of a child's environment (Downs, Moore, McFadden, & Costin, 2000).

Downs et al. (2000) note: "The field of child welfare is becoming known as *family and child services*. The field is vastly more complex than it was in the nineteenth and early twentieth century when our ancestors confidently responded to problems of family functioning by 'rescuing' children of poor or neglectful parents and placing them in institutions of one kind or another. Since then, for at least half a century, social changes have impelled child and family agencies to adapt and innovate services" (p. 2). The decisions have gone from removing children from their homes to working with children within the home and to providing services to families in which the child must grow and function.

The welfare of children is very important to me. Many children are both abused and neglected in their own homes. This is one reason that the family must be considered when addressing and assessing issues of child abuse and neglect. "In 1996 there were over three million reports of child abuse and neglect. Although three million reports were received, only about one in three cases were confirmed, after investigation, as victims of maltreatment, for a total of just under one million children" (Downs et al., 2000, p. 215). Although one million is less than three million, the number is still too high. And these are just the cases that are reported. What about the cases that are not reported? Families are in desperate need of intervention and support when it comes to caring for their children.

While writing this book I thought of the many abused and neglected children that I have come in contact with, and how they touched my life personally and professionally. I am often reminded of the tears in their eyes and the smiles on their faces when I walked into their homes. They were always welcoming and without a doubt they were always grateful for my intervention, even if it meant they had a temporary change in environment that was for their safety and well-being. I will never forget Andy, a 4-year-old boy who opened the door to his house one rainy day as I was making a visit to his home for suspected neglect of him and his little sister, April. When I walked into the house Andy said, "Do you want my mommy?" He went into the living room and attempted to wake her up from what seemed to be a deep sleep. She woke up and greeted me, and then told me that she had just fallen to sleep. It appeared that she had slept in her clothing all night.

Andy's mother went into another room to get their shot records. While she was away, Andy picked up his baby sister, who was only 8 months old, walked over to me and whispered in my ear, "Hey lady, do you want a boy and a girl?" Andy went on to say, "I am a good mommy and we are good." Andy was suggesting that I take him and his sister with me. I did everything in my power not to show how his statement affected me. I fought the tears as I talked to Andy's mother. She was 18 years old and had a substance abuse problem. She had grown up in a single-parent home with very little parental supervision, because her mother worked two jobs to keep them off welfare. She was 14 when she had Andy and dropped out of school. She had been an A student and had high hopes of going to college. After she had Andy, however, she lost her focus and became involved with a man who turned her on to crack cocaine.

There are far too many young mothers like this one—ill-prepared and often overwhelmed by parenthood—who may find themselves emotionally abusing their children (Crosson-Towers, 1998). Parents who emotionally abuse their children are often not happy with their lives. They are generally frustrated, disappointed, and have unmet emotional needs of their own (Crosson-Towers, 1998).

"Family structure also plays an important part in cases of child abuse. Single parents are more likely to abuse their children than are parents who live together. Abuse in single-parent families appears to be linked to poverty and may be explained by the stresses of living at very low income levels. Single fathers are more prone to abusing their children in poor, single-father households. Gelles (1989) found that these fathers have a rate of severe violence toward their children—406 per 1,000, a rate higher than for any other group of parents" (Downs et al., 2000, p. 241). It has been noted that younger children are at higher risk of being abused or neglected (Downs et al., 2000). Andy was only 4, and his sister was 8 months old.

Andy made me believe even more strongly in what I am commissioned to do by the profession of social work. In my ten years of practice in child welfare I met many just like Andy, and they reminded me that the field of child welfare desperately needs committed practitioners. The focus of intervention must be the family, and not just the individual child(ren). Nichols and Schwartz (1998) note that "changing a family changes the life of each of its members. Therefore, improvement can be lasting because each and every family member is changed and continues to exert synchronous change on each other" (p. 6). Although Andy was not physically abused, the emotional abuse and neglect that he and April suffered will be with them for the rest of their lives, and with the families they go on to create.

TYPES OF ABUSE

There are many types of abuse to children (physical, sexual, emotional, verbal, and neglect), and all too often these types overlap; generally, a child presents with more than one type of abuse. Definitions of abuse and neglect may vary based on different cultural values, socialization, family values, history, and political climate (Winston & Mara, 2001). Having an understanding of what constitutes various forms of abuse is crucial to assessing the safety of the child and the preservation of the family.

Physical Abuse

Physical abuse of children can be defined as nonaccidental injury inflicted on a child. The abuse is usually at the hands of a caretaker, but it can be perpetrated by another adult, or in some cases by an older child. Some protection agencies add the proviso that the abuse needs to have caused disfigurement, impairment of physical health, loss or impairment of a bodily organ, or substantial risk of death (Stein, 1991).

"In the consideration of what constitutes physical abuse, two dilemmas arise. The first is related to cultural context. Some cultures have customs or practices that child protection would consider abusive. For example, some Vietnamese families, in a ritual called *cdo gio*, rub their children with a coin heated to the point that it leaves burn marks. It is an intentional act, but designed, in that culture, to cure a variety of ills. Another dilemma for society is: what constitutes discipline and how is that differentiated from abuse? The physical punishment of children as a form of discipline has been practiced extensively throughout history in the United States. More recently, many parents are seeking alternatives to physical punishment in the raising of their children. There is still a significant number of parents who hit as a method of discipline. Some argue that what separates this type of discipline from abuse is a matter of degree. If bruises are left on a child and those bruises last for a prolonged period, the act is considered abusive" (Crosson-Towers, 1998, pp. 229–230).

"Society sanctions corporal punishment of children. Even though many people believe that any physical punishment of children is wrong and contributes to their emotional maladjustment, all states recognize the rights of parents to use physical force to discipline their children. The difficulty for those concerned with reporting child abuse is to differentiate between reasonable discipline and child abuse" (Downs et al., 2000, p. 241). Besharov (1990) provides guidelines for making this distinction: discipline may be considered unreasonable if a *"reasonably foreseeable consequence was or could have been the child's serious injury.* This includes any punishment that results in a broken bone, eye damage, severe welts, bleeding or any other injury that requires medical treatment" (p. 67). He points out that physical punishment of infants is always of concern, because infants are not developmentally able to understand the reason for the physical assault on them and because their soft tissues make any physical violence particularly dangerous. A forceful attack on the head of a child of any age is also dangerous and therefore defined as unreasonable punishment. In assessing cases of physical punishment, a number of factors should be considered, including "the child's age and physical and mental condition, the child's misconduct on the particular occasion and in the past, the parents' purpose, the kind and frequency of punishment inflicted, the degree of harm done to the child, and the type of location of the injuries" (Besharov, 1990, p. 68).

Neglect

Downs et al. (2000) state: "Not only is child neglect more prevalent than physical abuse, it is nearly as dangerous. About 45 percent of all child fatalities involve neglect. In spite of seriousness, child neglect has not received the media and scholarly attention accorded to child abuse. Furthermore, the attention given to neglect often focuses only on the observable physical harm. Neglect does often leave physical indications, but much of the damage from neglect accrues over time" (p. 235).

"The concept of neglect differs from culture to culture. In general, it is the role of parents to meet the physical and emotional needs of their offspring. These needs usually encompass shelter, food, clothing, medical care, educational needs, protection, supervision, and moral guidance. The manner in which these needs are met may differ, but failure to meet these basic human needs in some acceptable manner constitutes neglect" (Crosson-Towers, 1998, p. 236).

Emotional and Verbal Abuse

Winston and Mara (2001) state that "because emotional and psychological abuse are difficult to define, controversies regarding diagnostic procedures abound. The situation is complicated because these forms of abuse do not leave physical evidence, though they can be as devastating to the child or adolescent as physical abuse, sexual abuse, or neglect. Moreover, emotional and psychological abuse often take place in conjunction with other types of child maltreatment. In fact, some argue that psychological abuse is present in all forms of child maltreatment (Pearl, 1998). A child who is physically abused, sexually abused, or neglected is probably also being emotionally and psychologically abused. Even though multiple types of maltreatment often coexist, emotional and psychological abuse can occur separately" (p. 87).

Sexual Abuse

Sexual abuse refers to "contact with a child, where the child is being used for sexual stimulation by the other person" (Crosson-Towers, 1998, p. 240). Often the abuser is older than the child and has more power and/or resources. Because of the differences in age, power, and resources, the child is generally enticed or threatened into participating in the abuse. The abuse progresses, beginning with the least intrusive behaviors such as observation, or exposure to penile penetration. "During this progression, the abuser gauges the reactions of the child and grooms him/her for further abuse. In addition to being touched sexually or being compelled to touch the abuser, sexual abuse also includes in its definition the use of a child in the production of pornography or encouraging the child to view pornography or other sexual acts" (Crosson-Towers, 1998, p. 240).

According to Crosson-Towers (1998), "sexual abuse may be divided into several categories: incest or familial abuse, extra familial molestation, exploitation through pornography, prostitution, sex rings, or cults, and abuse within institutions" (p. 240).

ASSESSMENT AND INTERVENTION
IN CHILD ABUSE CASES

Accurately analyzing and assessing child abuse and neglect cases is vital to the safety of children and their families. If we as practitioners or child welfare professionals fail to assess the needs of the whole family, we lose opportunities for intervention, and we run the risk of misunderstanding the situation and the cultural context, which may put the children more at risk. The key role of assessment in case planning is obtaining good information and seeing that the whole picture is the only way to meet the family needs. The diagram in Figure 1.1 follows a client toward planned change using the generalist intervention model (Kirst-Ashman & Hull, 1999) and the problem-solving process. The steps are engagement, assessment, planning, implementation (treatment plan), follow-up, and termination. Let us use the following case vignette to understand the process in Figure 1.1.

The Crankfield Family.   *The client is a 23-year-old mother with six children, all under the age of 8. She has medical problems and is not sure she can provide for her children. Her husband left home six weeks ago and has decided that he no longer wants to be a husband or father. One year ago the Crankfields purchased their own home. Mrs. Crankfield is a stay-at-home mom, and her husband was the primary provider for the family. However, Mrs. Crankfield does have a college degree in accounting. When he left the family, Mr. Crankfield did not leave any money, and his whereabouts at this time are unknown. There are no extended family members in the area.*

Step One: Engagement

Engagement is the first step in the process of developing a relationship with a new client. In order for this process to work effectively, it is very important to meet the client and family where they are. Hepworth and Larson (1993) have pointed out this important fact: "A concept that guides practitioners in establishing and sustaining rapport and in maintaining psychological contact with clients is starting where the client is. Applying this concept to interviewing involves focusing attention on the immediate concerns and emotional states of clients" (p. 45).

In working with families, the practitioner must form a good working relationship with each member of the family. The practitioner should also remember that each family member is a unique individual. It is also important that family members are aware that their interaction with each other will impact the whole system. Students should remember that if they are

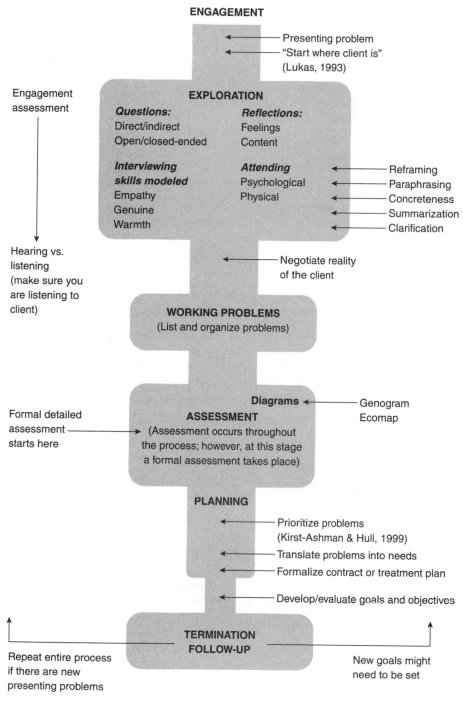

ENGAGEMENT

Presenting problem

"Start where client is"
(Lukas, 1993)

Engagement
assessment

EXPLORATION

Questions:
Direct/indirect
Open/closed-ended

Reflections:
Feelings
Content

*Interviewing
skills modeled*
Empathy
Genuine
Warmth

Attending
Psychological
Physical

Reframing
Paraphrasing
Concreteness
Summarization
Clarification

Hearing vs.
listening
(make sure you
are listening to
client)

Negotiate reality
of the client

WORKING PROBLEMS
(List and organize problems)

Formal detailed
assessment
starts here

Diagrams

Genogram
Ecomap

ASSESSMENT
(Assessment occurs throughout
the process; however, at this stage
a formal assessment takes place)

PLANNING

Prioritize problems
(Kirst-Ashman & Hull, 1999)

Translate problems into needs

Formalize contract or treatment plan

Develop/evaluate goals and objectives

**TERMINATION
FOLLOW-UP**

Repeat entire process
if there are new
presenting problems

New goals might
need to be set

FIGURE 1.1   The Planned Change Process

role-playing a case, it is very important to model genuineness, empathy, and authenticity.

After meeting the client, the next phase is to understand what is the presenting problem.

Presenting Problem.   The *presenting problem* is the reason you are in-volved with the client or family in the first place. According to Hepworth, Rooney, and Larsen (1997), "the presenting problem is highly significant because it reflects clients' immediate perception of the problem and is the focal point of clients' motivation for seeking help" (p. 205). It is therefore very important that a practitioner be aware of the difference between the presenting problem and the working problems. See Figure 1.1 on how to get from the presenting problem to the working problems.

Example: Client says, "I want to kill myself."

This is the presenting problem. There is very little you can do with a present-ing problem as you do not have enough information to make an assessment. That is why you move to the next phase of the interview, which is *exploration*.

Exploration.   Interviewing skills such as questions (open ended, closed ended, direct, and indirect), seeking concreteness, paraphrasing, clarifica-tion, reflection of feelings and content, summarization, and empathetic responding are used to explore reasons for the presenting problem. Through-out the interview, students should model genuineness, authenticity, and consciousness of attending skills, both physical and psychological.

Example: Worker—"How long have you felt this way?" (Closed-ended question)

"Tell me a little about what's been going on." (Open-ended question)

Summarization.   *Summarization* is often done throughout the exploration phase to make sure you are understanding what the client is saying. How-ever, summarization is particularly important when you are close to identi-fying the problems in the family, because it is at this point that you begin to make sense of what is actually happening with regard to family dynamics.

Negotiation of Reality.   *Negotiating reality* often occurs after you have sum-marized what you think the client has been saying. You and the client might not agree on what the problem is, and it is important that you and the client have a clear understanding of what is occurring in the family so that you are both working on the same issues. This phase is used when you are role-playing cases in class.

Defining the Working Problems. At this stage in the interview you have negotiated the reality of the client to make sure you and the client are in agreement. Now you and the client together *define what the working problems are.* In the case analysis you must assume that you have engaged with the client and therefore you can define the working problems based on the information given.

> *Example:* Worker—"Mrs. Crankfield, what do you see as the problems we can work on?"

Step Two: Assessment

Assessment is the second step in the process of doing a case analysis. According to Lukas (1993), "the purpose of the assessment phase is to help you make an accurate diagnosis, on the basis of which you can then formulate a conscientious treatment plan" (p. xii). Additionally, "social work practitioners must achieve more balanced perceptions of their clients by attuning themselves to strengths and potentialities as well as to dysfunction and pathology" (Hepworth et al., 1997, p. 198). Assessment is the "fluid and dynamic process that involves receiving, analyzing and synthesizing new information as it emerges during the entire course of a given case" (Hepworth et al., 1997, p. 196). As a product, assessment "involves an actual formulation or statement at a given time regarding the nature of the client's problems and other related factors" (Hepworth & Larsen, 1993, p. 193).

Assessment is an ongoing process. The more information you have about the client's situation, the more you will be able to direct your questions and understand what is occurring in the family. Sometimes a family history is so complex that it is important to use assessment diagrams to help explain the dynamics in the family system. In these instances we use assessment diagrams such as genograms and ecomaps.

Genograms

A genogram is a diagram of the family's generational configuration. It helps organize both historical and contemporary data on the major figures in the client's interpersonal environment. Thus, it helps the social worker understand how family patterns are affecting the current situation. Births, deaths, mental illness, alcoholism, divorce, separation, adoption, incest, and family occupation are examples of types of family data present on genograms, which provide a concise means for organizing complex and significant information helpful to intervention planning (Compton & Galaway, 1994, p. 383).

The following symbols may vary depending on their source. However, most of the time they are similar and signify family events and relationships. The names and ages of family members customarily are placed on the genogram, and a brief description of each family member is placed near his or her name.

○ = Female   □ = Male

▼ = Pregnancy   – – – = Marital separation

××= Death   ⋯⁄⋅⁄⋯ = Divorce

? = Whereabouts unknown

Figure 1.2 is a genogram of the Crankfield family, based on the information gathered so far from the mother and prepared after the initial session.

Ecomaps

An ecomap is a diagram of the family within its social context, and it includes the genogram. The purpose of the ecomap is to organize and clarify data on the supports and stresses in the family's environment. The major meso level and exo level social systems which affect the family are placed within circles. The family genogram is placed within the center circle (Compton & Galaway, 1994, p. 383).

The symbols for the ecomap may vary depending on the individual practioner, but for the most part they are similar:

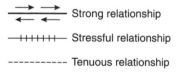

Strong relationship

————++++++—— Stressful relationship

----------- Tenuous relationship

No line at all means no relationship identified or revealed. Figure 1.3 is an initial ecomap of the Crankfield family.

Step Three: Planning

Planning is the third step in the process. Kirst-Ashman and Hull (1999) state that "goals are established to clarify the purpose of an intervention" (p. 223). Throughout this process, the practitioner must include the client. The clients

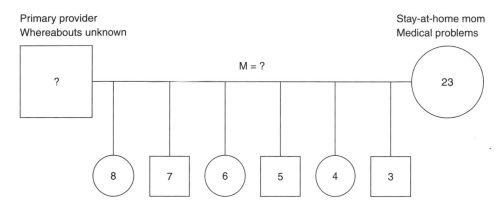

Primary provider
Whereabouts unknown

Stay-at-home mom
Medical problems

M = ?

?

23

8 7 6 5 4 3

FIGURE 1.2 Genogram of the Crankfield Family

must mutually agree on the goals established and the process by which those goals will be achieved. If the clients do not understand the goals or are not included in the process of setting the goals, chances are that the goals will not be accomplished.

Prioritize Problems. At this phase in the interview one needs to prioritize the problems, because some problems are more important than others and need immediate attention—for example, food for the children and money for the mortgage payment. Once you have prioritized the problems, you will be ready to turn those problems into needs and then proceed with the planning process. Let us take another look at the problems present in the Crankfield family. What are the needs?

PROBLEM	NEEDS
No income to care for family	Locate financial resources
Can't locate father	Locate the father to find out his intentions in caring for his family
No one to care for children if the mother seeks employment	Day care or some form of child care

Step Four: Treatment Plan

The fourth step in the generalist problem-solving process is to prepare a *treatment plan.* The type of treatment plan that seems to "be the most relevant and promising means of achieving the goals posited in the contract"

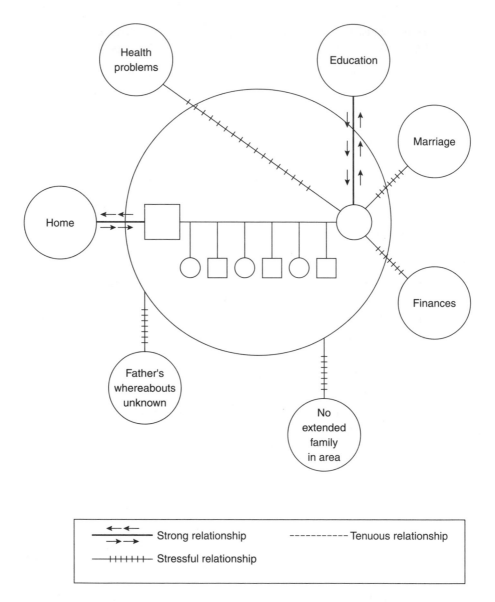

FIGURE 1.3   Ecomap of the Crankfield Family

is the task-centered system (Hepworth et al., 1997, p. 373). The first task in the task-oriented system is to partialize the goals. Hepworth et al. (1997) state that these "tasks may consist of either behavioral or cognitive actions that require effort (and often discomfort) on the clients' part" (p. 373). As each subgoal is reached, it should be evaluated. A new subgoal is then established, and so on until the overall goal is reached.

Step Five: Evaluation, Termination, and Follow-Up

The final step in the process of doing a case analysis includes *evaluation, termination, and follow-up.* Kirst-Ashman and Hull (1999) state that "to be effective as a social worker, you must know whether or not the interventions you employ are working" (p. 296). Therefore, developing effective evaluation strategies to track your interventions is very important. The process of evaluating your interventions should be ongoing, because it is important to know what is working and what is not working. Kirst-Ashman and Hull (1999) say, "being familiar with a variety of techniques to evaluate direct practice is important. Among the most common are single-subject designs, goal attainment scaling, task-achievement scaling, and client satisfaction questionnaires" (p. 308).

Termination is the end of the professional client relationship and of the planned change process. The management of this phase in the relationship is key to clients' success in being able to manage their own problems. I call this the empowerment phase. It is very important for clients to know that they have strengths that will sustain them without my intervention. Kirst-Ashman and Hull (1999) say that "termination must be based upon clear evidence that the goals and objectives have been achieved. Assisting the client in considering if termination is appropriate given actual progress is helpful" (p. 324). It is important to note that not all terminations are planned. Some are unplanned, for a number of reasons that depend on the circumstances.

Lastly, follow-up with a client allows you to learn how the client is functioning after your professional relationship has ended. Follow-up is not usually done in child welfare cases unless a case comes again to the attention of social services, perhaps because the child has again been victimized.

The following case demonstrates how the case analysis should work. The Johnson case was analyzed by an undergraduate student. The case will take you through each phase of the family case analysis using the questions at the end of each chapter. This case is intended only to give you an idea of how another undergraduate student analyzed the case; your formulation might be different, but equally useful.

EXAMPLE CASE STUDY: THE JOHNSON FAMILY

Engagement

My client is Henry Johnson, age 12, one of my youth diversion group members. Henry has been sent to my program because he has been involved with a group of youth vandalizing the neighborhood school. In addition, some of the boys were possessing marijuana.

Since this is the first time Henry has ever gotten into trouble as far as anyone knows, I wanted to find out about Henry and what might be happening in his life that might influence his behavior. I want to look at Henry's family dynamics, their structure and coping mechanisms. Henry is a unique individual, yet only a subsystem to a much larger system, his family and social environment.

Approximately two years ago Henry's father suffered a severe on-the-job accident which almost resulted in death. As a result of the accident, Henry Johnson's family underwent many changes. For instance, Henry's grades immediately started to slip after the accident. He was close with his father and they used to enjoy many activities together. However, since the accident his father is seldom home, and when he is, he is short-tempered. As a result, it appears Henry has looked for companionship outside the house with his peers. Everyone in the family seemed to fall apart or fragment only after the accident and the change in their father.

It is clear to me that the working problems are much more involved than Henry's presenting problem. Every individual in Henry's family felt the impact of Mr. Johnson's accident. Therefore, not only Henry, but his entire family is in need of assistance.

Mr. Johnson remains a crucial part of the family system, especially to Henry, who needs a father figure and male role model. Henry and his parents need to be alerted to the possibility that Henry's recent behavior could be a small symptom to a bigger problem. Empathy and reflective listening may help Mr. and Mrs. Johnson see how Mr. Johnson's accident has snowballed into a multitude of problems impacting everyone in the family. Empowerment concerning the family's strength and determination in their time of crisis may give the Johnsons a boost of encouragement. Throughout the hard times, this family has physically stayed together, but cohesion and structure has diminished.

Assessment

There are three working problems within the Johnson family that stand out: Henry's father's ability to cope since the accident; the family's reaction to the accident; and the family's shift in roles. Therefore, a family assessment, treatment plan, and intervention are necessary, which includes Henry's parents, siblings, and grandmother. Figure 1.4 is a genogram/ecomap of the Johnson family which illustrates the facts and patterns occurring in the family. Figure 1.5 is an ecomap of the Johnson family which illustrates the family within its social context and displays the dynamics that are occurring in the family.

As a professional social worker, I can assume that Mr. Johnson may have feelings of depression and/or despair concerning his accident and the

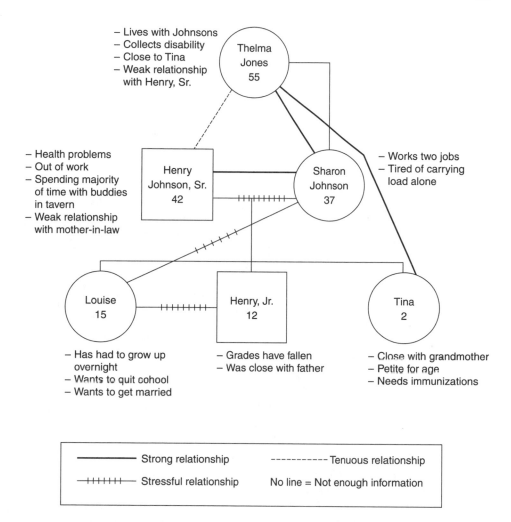

- Lives with Johnsons
- Collects disability
- Close to Tina
- Weak relationship with Henry, Sr.

Thelma Jones 55

- Health problems
- Out of work
- Spending majority of time with buddies in tavern
- Weak relationship with mother-in-law

Henry Johnson, Sr. 42

Sharon Johnson 37

- Works two jobs
- Tired of carrying load alone

Louise 15

Henry, Jr. 12

Tina 2

- Has had to grow up overnight
- Wants to quit school
- Wants to get married

- Grades have fallen
- Was close with father

- Close with grandmother
- Petite for age
- Needs immunizations

——————— Strong relationship   - - - - - - - - - Tenuous relationship

+++++++— Stressful relationship   No line = Not enough information

FIGURE 1.4   Genogram/Ecomap of the Johnson Family

resulting change in lifestyle he has had to undergo. He is no longer the provider for his family, the one thing his mother-in-law respected him for. He may feel as though he's let her down as well as her daughter. He may look to his buddies at the tavern as an escape from his home life.

Henry's parents seem to be a weak subsystem. Henry probably looked to his friends for companionship and a sense of belonging. He does not seem to have a specified role in his family system. His mother is always working, his grandmother is interested in Tina, Louise tries to boss him around, and his dad is seldom home.

Henry must be feeling isolated and alone. He's left to take care of himself without much guidance. As a professional social worker, I realize peer

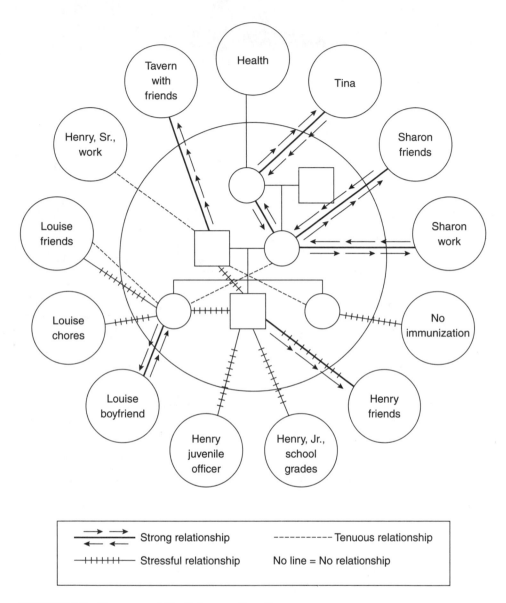

Strong relationship   Tenuous relationship

Stressful relationship   No line = No relationship

FIGURE 1.5   Ecomap of the Johnson Family

pressure can be overwhelming, especially to adolescents. He probably feels his group of friends is the most positive thing he has going for him.

Henry probably misses his relationship with his father. Mr. Johnson is not missed only for his earning capabilities, but for his leadership as the head of the family. It's very important that Mr. Johnson realize his family needs him, and he is just as capable of giving to them today as he was two years ago—emotionally, if not physically.

As I delve even deeper into this situation, I realize Mr. Johnson may be drinking or even abusing alcohol when he's with his buddies. Alcohol may be an obstacle in reaching our goals. In addition, Henry, Jr., may have been one of the boys who was caught with marijuana. Counseling or treatment concerning substance abuse may be necessary. I realize that drugs and alcohol can be detrimental both to the user as well as members of the family.

Individuals within the family system may not be willing to communicate or work together. Resistance by members may be a barrier to family intervention success. Who is resisting and how they resist can also be very helpful in understanding the Johnson family dynamics. It is very important to have everyone participate, because one individual can have an effect on the entire family.

It was crucial to find out about Mr. Johnson's accident and his roles in the family both before and after the accident. It's important to be aware of the family's restructure in their time of crisis. It was also very important to understand that Henry was very close with his father before the accident. I believe this combination of events sets the stage for Henry's presenting problem.

The Johnson family is not without strengths. They are a two-parent family. The mother, Sharon Johnson, is healthy and capable of working. The grandmother is a strength because she could step in to care for Tina, who needed lots of attention as a baby. Also, Henry's parents want Henry to succeed in this program or he'll have to face the consequences of juvenile justice or child welfare. They may be persuaded to get involved in family services in order to keep him out of further trouble.

I think Henry would be motivated toward having his family function as it did before his father had his accident. Henry's parents may be resistant to help at first, since they didn't do anything wrong; it was their son who needed assistance. But I must use my skills to trigger their emotions to remember how their family functioned before the accident. I must instill hope in Henry and his parents that the entire family can once again become stable, secure, and supportive. I want to help the family members see how the last two years have put a tremendous strain on the entire family which has led to a multitude of problems. With the help of the entire family, they can also get out of this situation and begin to function as a family again; everyone pulling for the good of the whole. I must empathize with the struggles and hardships they have all had to undergo and compliment them on how well they did manage to pull through in their crisis.

Another alternative is to confront Mr. Johnson with the undesirable consequences his family will face if he does not make an effort to get involved: his family may fall apart because Sharon is tired of carrying the full load alone; Henry, Jr., may be heading for the juvenile justice system; Louise may get pregnant so she can drop out of school and get married; and Tina may not receive proper medical care.

Planning

Primary Goal: To restore equilibrium and cohesion within the Johnson family system.   There are subgoals and objectives along with individual tasks that will aid in obtaining our primary goal. By prioritizing and partializing, the success of priority goals may eliminate the need for several existing goals. There are also individual tasks involved with each goal and objective. To ensure a more successful outcome of our tasks, it is important to rehearse them and discuss possible obstacles.

I feel that family therapy with Henry, Sr., as my first focus is the best strategy. Henry, Sr., doing his part to help support his family is crucial. By starting with Mr. Johnson, I believe the entire family will benefit. Mrs. Johnson may not feel she's struggling alone; Louise, in turn, may not have to carry an adult role in the family, Henry can reopen his relationship with his father, and Thelma won't be needed as live-in help. Second, I want to focus on the parental subsystem. A strong parental subsystem helps to ensure stability and structure in the family system. Finally, the entire family will be counseled. When Mrs. Johnson and each member of the family is added to the counseling session with Mr. Johnson, we begin with a new baseline and select the treatment in relation to the new group. This is known as the multiple baseline design.

Goal/Objective: Alleviate emotional distress Mr. Johnson may be experiencing since his accident due to identity transformation and role change. The objective is to have Mr. Johnson function as a vital part of the family system once again.

TASKS (Who will do what? When? and how to measure success)
1. Mr. Johnson will attend counseling on role loss, social transition, and coping strategies, within 1 wk. Successful if he attends counseling.
2. Mr. Johnson will make appointment with local clinic for 2nd medical opinion regarding existing problems within 2 days. Successful if he makes appointment.

Goal/Objective: Enhance communication between Henry, Sr., and Sharon. The objective is to build a strong parental subsystem within the family system.

TASKS
1. Henry, Sr., will share one positive statement regarding his relationship with Sharon within 2 days. Successful if he shares positive statement.
2. Sharon will share one positive statement regarding her relationship with Henry, Sr., within 2 days. Successful if she shares positive statement.

3. Mrs. Johnson will attend counseling on social transition and strategies within 1 wk. Successful if she attend counseling.

Goal/Objective: Obtain financial assistance and resources. The objective is to ease some of the financial burden Sharon is carrying alone.

TASKS

1. Henry, Sr., will call the number from social worker concerning job training and placement services within one week. Successful if he makes the phone call.
2. Sharon will call the number from social worker concerning financial assistance (both cash and in-kind services) within one week. Successful if she makes the phone call.
3. Sharon will contact local clinic on 14th and Olive concerning immunization for Tina. Successful if she contacts the clinic.

Goal/Objective: Restore relationship between Henry and his father. The objective is to build self-worth and provide a male role model and father figure for Henry.

TASKS

1. Henry will spend 15 minutes with his father for the next three days. Successful is they meet each day.
2. Henry, Sr., will spend 15 minutes with his son for the next three days. Successful if they meet each day.
3. Henry will tell his father what he misses most in their relationship within the next three days. Successful if Henry tells his father.

To evaluate the progress in obtaining our goals, I want to elicit feedback from my clients as well as explore my professional views. If my clients appear disappointed and discouraged at the lack of results, we can certainly be flexible in reviewing our tasks and establishing new obtainable goals. As the professional, however, it is important to empower my clients and point out the accomplishments they have made, however small, that they may not notice. I will monitor and evaluate progress as negotiated in the contract (see contract in Figure 1.6).

Lukas (1993) states that in conducting our first interview with a child, we should ask ourselves: "Why now? What are the current pressures or changes in the life of the child that are causing attention to be drawn to [him or her] at this moment? Is the change that has occurred a change in the child, or is it a change in the circumstances surrounding [him or her]" (p. 59). Lukas (1993) also supports the idea that symptoms may appear in

FIGURE 1.6   Contract/Treatment Plan

Client: Henry Johnson and his family (includes Mrs. Jones)

I. Brief Description of the Problem:
Henry Johnson was caught vandalizing with a group of youth. For the last two years his family has had to restructure due to his father's severe on-the-job accident, which left him unemployed without compensation. Mr. Johnson escapes to the local tavern to avoid his family situation. He must define a new role for himself in the family system.

II. Primary Goal(s):
A. Restore equilibrium and cohesion within the Johnson family system
B. Alleviate motional stress Mr. Johnson may be experiencing
C. Enhance communication between Mr. and Mrs. Johnson
D. Obtain financial assistance
E. Restore relationship between Henry and his father

III. We, the undersigned, agree to the objectives in the following plan:
A. Mr. Johnson will cooperate as necessary in order to function as a vital part of the family system once again.
B. Mr. and Mrs. Johnson will work toward building a strong parental subsystem within the family system.
C. Mr. and Mrs. Johnson will take necessary steps to increase household income.
D. Build Henry, Jr.'s, self-worth and provide a male role model and father figure for him.

IV. Evaluation of Progress:
Task evaluation will be conducted at the beginning of each counseling session or at least within two or three sessions. We will discuss the success or failure of assigned tasks. We will discuss the strategies used for success as well as confront the obstacles that may have interfered. As we progress toward goal attainment, we can shift our focus to new goals and tasks. If current strategies for success are not working, we may need to try something different.

_____   _____
                                         (Signature of Social Worker)
_____

_____

(Signature(s) of Client(s))

_____   _____

(Date)   (Date)

five places within the family: "one of the parents, between the parents, between a parent and a child, between children, and one of the children" (p. 45). In Henry's situation, it was clear to see that both of these statements hold true. Henry was feeling the stress and emptiness his family was undergoing. Now that he is in a group program for troubled youth, there is an opportunity to treat the root of the problem, his family situation.

Kirst-Ashman and Hull (1999) emphasize the family's significance concerning individual members' physical and emotional well-being. The healthy family system functions with appropriate boundaries and subsystems, family norms (rules specifying proper behavior), family roles, a balance of power within the family and among its members, and intergenerational knowledge concerning impact on family functioning. Henry, Sr., has had to live with constant pain and breathing problems since the accident which he feels keeps him from full-time work. He may need someone to talk to concerning his health, and more importantly, the social, emotional, and physical changes that have evolved due to his accident.

As roles change within families, it is important that parents redefine their expectations for each other. It seems Mr. and Mrs. Johnson never sat down to redefine family roles. Mr. Johnson could only think that he was useless to everyone because he no longer was the provider of his family. This is clearly Mr. Johnson's view or belief of himself. He has filled his head with misconceptions of himself and as a result has changed his behavior accordingly. Hepworth and Larsen (1993) illustrate how cognitive therapy can help "clients to differentiate between feelings and cognitions" (p. 424). Cognitive restructuring helps the clients remove barriers to change and foster willingness to risk new behaviors. Mr. Johnson, with the help of counseling and education, can begin to understand how dysfunctional, negative thoughts can produce self-defeating behavior and thoughts.

Kirst-Ashman and Hull (1999), Lukas (1993), and Hepworth and Larsen (1993) all support the ideology that family therapy derives from "systems theory" and assumes communication is circular, wherein every action produces a reaction. Mr. Johnson's accident impacted everyone in the family system. His mother-in-law came to live in his house, his wife took on a second job, his oldest daughter became responsible for all household duties, Henry lost his father's companionship and role model, and Tina has missed immunizations due to finances.

I drew concepts from systems theory, as well as small group theory. Generational subsystems, spousal subsystems, and sibling subsystems are all vital parts to the system at large. A family's main objective is to provide an environment and the necessary resources for the healthy development of all members.

Longres (1990) discusses "one of the primary functions of the family which is providing affection and emotional stability." He also states "social workers should focus on ways to maintain and improve emotional support, nurturance, and bonding among family members" (p. 198). There did not seem to be much stability in the Johnson family since the accident. Emotions seemed either to peak or dive—both were negative. There did not seem to be much affection and laughter in Henry's family.

Lukas (1993) believes it is important to remind our clients of better times and the value of recapturing those healthy moments and feelings prior to the crisis. My strategy was to get to the father's emotions by reminding him of their family before the accident. He was close with his son. Both of them may miss that closeness and need each other now more than ever.

It's imperative to have Henry, Sr., realize his self-determination in this situation. I will empathize with how Henry, Sr., feels about his accident and life before the accident as compared to the present. However, it's time to face reality. It appears Henry, Sr., looked to his buddies when he felt he was worthless—no job, poor health, not providing for his family. Reality is that Henry, Sr., is a very important part of this family structure, before the accident and today.

REFERENCES

Besharov, D. J. (1990). *Recognizing Child Abuse: A Guide for the Concerned.* New York: The Free Press.

Compton, B., & Galaway, B. (1994). *Social Work Processes,* 5th ed. Pacific Grove, CA: Brooks/Cole.

Crosson-Towers, C. (1998). *Exploring Child Welfare: A Practice Perspective.* Boston: Allyn & Bacon.

Downs, S. W., Moore, E., McFadden, E. J., & Costin, L. B. (2000). *Child Welfare and Family Services: Policies and Practice,* 6th ed. Boston: Allyn & Bacon.

Gelles, R. J. (1989). Child abuse and violence in single-parent families: Parent absence and economic deprivation. *American Journal of Orthopsychiatry, 59*(4), 492–501.

Hepworth, D. H., & Larsen, J. A. (1993). *Direct Social Work Practice: Theory and Skills,* 4th ed. Pacific Grove, CA: Brooks/Cole.

Hepworth, D., Rooney, R., & Larsen, J. (1997). *Direct Social Work Practice: Theory and Skills,* 5th ed. Pacific Grove, CA: Brooks/Cole.

Kirst-Ashman, K. K., & Hull, G. H. (1999). *Understanding Generalist Practice,* 2nd ed. Chicago: Nelson-Hall.

Lukas, S. (1993). *Where to Start and What to Ask: An Assessment Handbook.* New York: W. W. Norton.

Nichols, M. P. & Schwartz, R. C. (1998). *Family Therapy: Concepts and Methods.* Boston: Allyn & Bacon.

Pearl, P. S. (1998). Psychological abuse. In J.A. Monteleone & A.E. Brodeur (Eds.), *Child Maltreatment: A Clinical Guide and Reference* (2nd ed., pp. 371–396). St. Louis: G. W. Medical Publishing.

Stein, T. J. (1991). *Child Welfare and the Law.* New York: Longman.

Webb, N. B. (1996). *Social Work Practice with Children.* New York: The Guilford Press.

Winoton, M. A., & Mara, B. A. (2001). *Child Abuse & Neglect: Multidisciplinary Approaches.* Boston: Allyn & Bacon.

CHAPTER TWO

PHYSICAL ABUSE

THE MATHIS FAMILY

Student Instructions

You are an ongoing protective services worker and you have just been assigned to investigate the Mathis family further and decide what should happen to the children. You are also required to assess the situation and prepare a long-term plan for this family. Mrs. Mathis was diagnosed with paranoid schizophrenia after the birth of Devin. She recognizes that she needs inpatient treatment but is concerned about who will take care of her children. According to the initial report from the protective services investigator, there is some extended family. The case has been referred to you for further investigation and assessment of the situation.

Family Composition

The Mathis family consists of a single mother with four children. Mrs. Catherine Mathis is a 30-year-old African American woman. She is married to Paul Mathis, who abandoned them about three years ago. She thinks they might have gotten a divorce but says that she is not sure, because she has just tried to block all of her bad memories out of her mind. She remembers signing some papers he sent to the house about a year ago, but she is not sure what the papers were. She has two daughters, Denise Smith, age 15, and Devin Mathis, age 12. She has two sons, Marcus Mathis, age 8, and Benjamin Mathis, age 6. Mrs. Mathis's mother, Cassie Kelly, is involved in the family but does not live in the home.

Current Situation

The Department of Children and Family Services (DCFS) received a call from Denise's school stating that Mrs. Mathis had recently lost control with her daughters, Denise and Devin, and beat them with a belt. A teacher at Denise's school saw the marks and reported it to the principal, and he called DCFS. The local mental health agency also received a call from Mrs. Mathis. She stated that she was feeling sick again and that she had beat her two oldest children but had not meant to hurt them. She also stated that she did not want to lose her children, but she thought she needed to be hospitalized for a few days. Mrs. Mathis is known to the local mental health agency, as she and her ex-husband have a long history of mental illness. The report stated that Mrs. Mathis beat Denise and Devin with a belt and left several severe marks on their bodies. The report of physical abuse was confirmed, but the case is still being investigated.

Family Background

Mrs. Mathis's job pays little more than minimum wage and she has to do what she can to make ends meet for the family. Her annual income is $15,000.00 per year. The family resides in a rural county in Georgia with a population of about 8,000 people. Everyone knows everyone, and it is very important to Mrs. Mathis that her family remains intact, because people had thought she would not make it after her husband left. She has three brothers and four sisters. Three of her siblings and her mother live in the same city.

Mrs. Mathis is renting a two-bedroom house into which she and the children moved after her husband left. She states that they need more space, but this is all that she can afford at this time. She says the house is in need of repairs, as the floor in the bathroom is caving in. She has asked the landlord to fix the floor, but he has not taken care of it yet. She is afraid that if she insists on him fixing it, he will put her and the children out of the house because when he rented the house to her, he thought she had only two children. The house is very clean, and Mrs. Mathis and the children take great pride in their home.

According to Mrs. Mathis, her husband is employed by the local department of sanitation. His annual income is about $35,000, but he does not give her any money to help support the children. She states that he is well liked at his job and in the community. He was the backbone of their family when he was with them and was a lot of support to her in raising the children. However, when he got sick, he left the home and did not return. Mrs. Mathis says that he too has suffered from mental illness and has had at least two nervous breakdowns. When he was with them, he was the president of the Parents' Association and very active in church. She goes on to say that she thinks he was overwhelmed by taking care of her and the children and now he is refusing to have any contact with them at all, even though he lives only two blocks from them. Mr. Mathis is not aware of the report of physical abuse and that Mrs. Mathis is sick again.

Denise

Denise is 15 years old and a very intelligent child. She sustained several marks to her legs, back, arms, and buttocks. She is not angry at her mother, because she knows that her mother is sick. She received a scholarship to attend a private high school and is an A student. She hopes to take precollege courses and would like to become a psychiatrist someday. She is very outgoing and has a lot of friends. She would like to go away to college, but is afraid that her mother might not be able to manage without her.

Mr. Mathis is not Denise's biological father, but she calls him "Daddy" because he is the only father she knows. She hopes that one day she can meet her biological father, because she has overheard Mr. Mathis say to her mother that he should not have to be responsible for her because she is not his child. She cannot believe that her "Daddy" walked out on them, because he was the one who kept everything going. However, she adds that her mother is trying to do a good job and the children are afraid that one day somebody might take them away from their mother. Denise also received a scholarship to go to Europe and is scheduled to leave in three months, but is wondering if she should go, because her younger siblings depend on her so much. She forgives her mother for the belt beating and does not want DCFS involved in their family business.

Devin

Devin is 12 years old and very quiet. She sustained several marks to her back and severe marks to her buttocks, and it is very difficult for her to sit down. She is a little upset with her mother because they were just at the library getting some books. She did not disclose much to the protective services investigator, but did state that she did not want to be removed from the home, because her mother needed them. She is also a smart student and is in special education at the local public school. According to her teachers and her mother, she is not very outgoing—she is somewhat of a loner. She feels bad that her mother got sick after she was born. She enjoys watching TV and reading novels. She gets along with both parents but seems to take more responsibility for her mother since her father left the home. She says that she does not really care whether he returns. She really admires her sister, Denise, and wishes she could be just like her. She loves music, but very quiet music. She considers Denise her one and only friend.

Marcus

Marcus is 8 years old and has Down syndrome. He also attends public school and is in a special education program. According to the school officials, Marcus is very high-functioning and really likes school. Marcus was not whipped, and it is not known whether Mrs. Mathis has ever abused him. He is sort of shy but smiles a lot. When asked who his mother was, he said "Denise." According to Denise, she takes care of him and she has always gone to the school and talked to the teachers for her mother.

Benjamin

Benjamin is 6 years old and very bright. He is in public school, and according to school officials he is doing quite well. He is very healthy and does not seem to really know what is going on. He seems to identify Denise as "Mama" too. He does not know much about his father, because Mr. Mathis left the house when he was 2 years old. During the home visit, he sat on Mrs. Mathis's lap and hugged her, and it appeared that he was being very protective of her.

Extended Family

Cassie Kelly is Mrs. Mathis's mother. She lives about 10 miles away from her daughter and grandchildren. She is originally from north Georgia but moved near her daughter after her daughter became ill. Since moving, she has made a lot of friends and is planning to go on a field mission with some other senior citizens for one year. She is really excited about the mission, but she only decided to go because she thought her daughter and children were managing better. She has rented her house out to a new family in town for the year that she plans to be gone. The new family is scheduled to move in two months from now. Mrs. Kelly is very concerned about her daughter and grandchildren. She states that her daughter loves the children and she cannot believe that her daughter whipped the girls, because she has never done this before. She is very angry at her son-in-law, because he will not help out with the children and this has put more pressure on her daughter.

Mrs. Kelly would like to help her family get situated, because she has just received her assignment. She is being sent to India to work in an orphanage for poor children This trip is a lifelong dream. Everything has been approved, and she is scheduled to leave in two months. She is not willing to give up her dream, although she realizes that her daughter is very dependent on her. She is not sure why her daughter has suddenly become sick. She has asked her what happened, but her daughter does not seem to be able to tell her. She definitely thinks that intervention is needed for her grandchildren. She hopes they will not be taken away from her daughter. She also states that she wishes all of her other children were close. However, she says that her other children have never understood Catherine, and she is not sure they would be willing to help out while she is gone, because they have so many problems of their own.

THE WONG FAMILY

Student Instructions

You are an intact family worker with the State Department of Children and Family Services. You have just received the Wong case. The Wong family has been reported for alleged physical abuse. This is the first incident reported since the Le children were placed with the Wongs. The parents also seem to be experiencing other problems with Chu, Lee, and Mia.

Family Composition

The Wong family consists of the father, Mr. Chang Wong, age 35, and his wife, Mrs. Wu Wong, age 33. They have four foster children, two sons and two daughters: Chu Le, age 9, Lee Le, age 7, Mia Le, age 5, and Wae Le, age 3. The family also has a pet bird, named Bertie. The family lives in a supportive community where the neighbors are predominately Asian. Neither of the parents has family members in the United States, although Mr. Wong hopes to bring his parents to the United States in another year. However, the Wongs have received a lot of support from their sponsors, Mr. and Mrs. Leftish. They have not returned to China since arriving to the United States.

Current Situation

Mr. Wong spanked his foster son, Lee. Lee sustained welts and bruises on his lower back and bruises on the back of his legs. Mr. Wong stated that he was not trying to hurt Lee, but was angry when he spanked the boy. Lee was very disruptive in school and in the last month has been very disobedient. They have had a difficult time communicating with him and they have tried several punishments, none of which seemed to work. Lee was spanked after repeated calls from his teacher about his refusal to do his school work. The teacher states that he is either playing or daydreaming, and is having a difficult time focusing on his work.

Family Background

Mr. and Mrs. Wong came to the United States after they graduated from college. They were sponsored by a missionary couple from Maine. They have been in the United States for ten years. They have tried to have children but have been unsuccessful. About three years ago they decided to consider adoption. They were encouraged by friends in their church, who had adopted two children. They were a little apprehensive about adopting children because this is not common in the Chinese community. However, their sponsors encouraged them and they proceeded with the paperwork. About two-and-a-half years ago they received a call stating that four Chinese American siblings had been abandoned by their mother and needed a temporary foster home. They agreed to take the children. The children have been in their home for almost three years now, and they are hoping to adopt the children. The whereabouts of the mother and father are still unknown. The case worker has been unsuccessful in contacting them. The case worker did locate an address for the grandparents in China and has sent several letters but has not received any correspondence from them. The history that the department has been able to construct about the children came directly from them, their birth certificates, Chu's last school records, and conversations with his teachers.

The children told the case worker and the police that their parents left for China. Chu stated that his father left first and then his mother went to China to look for their father. According to Chu, his mother took them to the police station and told them that the police would find them a home. She also told them that she might not be able to return for them until they were "big." All of the children were born in the United States and are U.S. citizens, and none of the children speaks Chinese.

The Department of Children and Family Services is providing a foster care subsidy and medical health services for each child and will continue to do so until the children are 18 years old or have been adopted. Mr. Wong is employed full time as an accountant, and Mrs. Wong is a stay-at-home mom. The family is involved in the local Roman Catholic church. The family is very active in cultural events and are very close to each other. The foster parents use denial of privileges, verbal admonishment, and time outs as forms of discipline. However, Mr. Wong has admitted spanking the boys on a couple of occasions.

Wu Wong

Mrs. Wong was born in China. She has dark hair, brown eyes, and wears glasses. She has two siblings, both still residing in China. Her father owned a business but became ill and died of cancer two years ago. Mrs. Wong has been very sad since his death, because she was financially unable to return to China for his funeral. Also, she did not feel comfortable leaving the children and she did not want them to think she would not return from China for them. Her mother has suffered from clinical depression since her father died. She would love to bring her mother to the United States, but Mr. Wong must bring his parents first, because his father has been diagnosed with lung cancer and the Wongs hope they can get treatment for him here.

Chang Wong

Mr. Wong was also born in China. He has brown eyes and gray-black hair. He has one older brother in China. His brother is physically disabled, and his parents have taken care of him all his life. Three years ago his brother got married and now resides with his wife. It was very difficult for his parents to let his brother go, and they were not very supportive of the marriage. Then, shortly after his brother got married, his father was diagnosed with cancer. Mr. Wong feels very responsible for his whole family and is working very hard to bring his parents to the United States. His parents are hesitant about leaving China because of their other son, and they hope to return there after treatment.

Mr. Wong says that he is committed to Lee and the other children. He feels very bad about the spanking he gave Lee because he thinks the children have been through enough. Mr. Wong has stated that at least he doesn't spank them all of the time. On one occasion he admits that he slapped Chu and Lee. He states he has not hit the girls at all. Mrs. Wong says she would rather not use corporal punishment, but her husband makes the decisions about discipline.

Chu

Chu, age 9, has brown eyes, dark black hair, and a dimple in his left jaw. He says that he looks like his father. Chu was 6 years old when his mother abandoned them, and he remembers his parents very well. He is very sad and thinks of traveling to China to locate his mother someday. He thinks his mother was either lost or does not have money to return to get them. He does not bond well with others and is not close to the Wongs at all. Chu is very upset about Lee being spanked. He has not verbalized his feelings to the Wongs, but he has told his reading teacher that his father is "mean" sometimes. Chu was never in favor of the adoption, because he always felt his mother might come back and get them.

Lee

Lee is 7 years old and very friendly. He has dark black hair, light brown eyes, and wears glasses. Lee is very active and has a problem with his attention span. He loves school but misses his mother. Although Lee seems to have bonded with Mrs. Wong, he was very close to his mother. He listens to Chu and almost sees Chu as his father.

Mia

Mia is 5 years old. Mia was 2 when her mother left them, and she doesn't speak of her mother at all. She was not attached to her. She has bonded well with Mr. Wong but does not communicate with Mrs. Wong. This is a problem, because Mia cries whenever Mrs. Wong tries to hold her or comfort her. Mia is very friendly, but timid and shy. She loves music and puzzles. She enjoys being alone, and Mrs. Wong states that Mia is a loner and rarely talks or communicates her needs. Her teacher thinks she should be tested for possible developmental problems. However, the Wongs thinks she might grow out of her difficulties.

Wae

Wae is 3 years old, and she was a newborn when their mother abandoned them. She has bonded to both foster parents. They state that they feel very close to Wae, as if she were their own child. Wae is very happy and well adjusted.

THE ANDERSON FAMILY

Student Instructions

You are a social worker at a private child welfare agency. The Anderson family has just been referred to your agency for continued assessment and services. The family was initially referred to Families First, another private child welfare agency. Families First can no longer provide services to the Anderson family, and the Department of Children and Family Services (DCFS) is now contracting with your agency to continue serving this family. The family continues to have problems, but Families First was unable to continue to service them because of conflicts between several of the social workers and the mother. According to the record, the case worker and the mother could never agree on a treatment plan. Her oldest son, Kevin has just been admitted to the hospital, and the family problems seem to be escalating.

Family Composition

The Anderson family consists of a single African American mother with two sons, 6-year-old Kevin and 7-month-old Keith. Mrs. Valerie Anderson also has three of her siblings living with her: her brother, Richard Anderson, who is 32 years old; her sister, Priscilla Anderson, who is 34 years old; and her younger sister, Faith James, who is 14 years old. On occasions her mother, Geneva James, 52, and another sister, Latrice James, 18, also live with her. According to Mrs. Anderson, they are in and out because sometimes they stay with their boyfriends.

Presenting Problem

Child Protective Services referred the Anderson family to Families First for services. An investigation of Valerie Anderson had just been completed, indicating lack of supervision, risk of harm, and cuts, welts, and bruises. The injuries were sustained by her son Kevin, then 5 years old.

Kevin received bruises to the face, chest, arms, legs, and upper back. Kevin was playing in the street the following day. An anonymous male neighbor saw his lacerations and called the hotline, and the investigation began. Valerie admitted whipping Kevin with an extension cord. Kevin remained at home with his mother, with the provision that Priscilla Anderson, Kevin's maternal aunt, would supervise Valerie with the children. The family was then referred to Families First to avoid Kevin and Keith going into foster care.

Current Situation

Kevin is currently at Simpson Hospital being tested for attention deficit disorder, hyperactivity, psychotic illness, and brain damage. Dr. Dennis, Kevin's psychiatrist, is recommending medication to alter Kevin's inappropriate behaviors. Valerie is in full agreement regarding Kevin receiving medication. She has requested several times that Kevin receive medications "to obey me and calm down." The concern of the Families First therapist was that because of Valerie's limitations and her lack of knowledge as to appropriate use of medication, she will overmedicate Kevin.

Family Background

Valerie is 25 years old and has never been married. She has expressed a desire to stay home with her children because of Keith's age. She expresses no desire to work outside the home because she states that they can manage with public assistance and her medical payments. Generationally, this appears to be consistent with family norms. The only person who works outside the home in Valerie's family is her brother, who works part time. Valerie has stated that she would not mind babysitting in the home. Her sister, Priscilla, babysits five days a week in the home, and Richard works at Pizza Hut. For the most part, all five people in the home live on Valerie's income.

Kevin is not developing to his full potential. He cannot identify numbers, colors, letters of the alphabet, or geometric shapes. Kevin does not dress himself, groom himself, or tie his own shoes. His speech is not always clear, and he cannot write his own name. Because of his age, the Families First social worker was unable to determine Keith's level of development. Valerie's lack of patience, inconsistency, and lack of follow-through with guidance or verbal praise limits her ability to teach the children skills. When Kevin is unable to do something the first time, Valerie will make a negative comment ("See Kevin, Kelly can say her ABC's, you can't."). The social worker at Families First also noticed that the parenting skills of the other adults involved are also very limited. The other adults follow the same pattern, showing lack of verbal skills, limited patience, and inconsistency with Kevin.

Valerie receives food stamps and public aid for Kevin and Keith. Because of Valerie's developmental limitations, she receives supplementary Social Security Income (SSI). It was reported in the social history that Valerie has been diagnosed as mildly mentally disabled. Intellectually, Valerie appears to be limited. She often has difficulty reading and understanding what has been read. She also appears to have difficulty attending to tasks. Her youngest sister, Faith, is severely disabled, both mentally and physically.

Valerie has a strong system of support. The extended family also supports Valerie's ideas that Kevin has a problem and that he needs help. The family does not follow through with directives associated with a treatment plan. For example, when special treats were used as reinforcers for Kevin, the adults would give them to other children. Family members would give Kevin his reinforcers because he would ask repeatedly. Valerie once reported that she felt a discipline that would work for Kevin would be to lock him in his bedroom all day. Latrice, Valerie's sister, stated, "Time out will not work. He needs to be locked away somewhere."

The roles in Valerie's family are not defined and clear. The care-taking responsibilities as well as the disciplining of the children are done by all of the adults (Mrs. James, Priscilla, Richard, Valerie). It was reported by another social service agency involved with the family that on one occasion, Faith was instructed to keep Keith quiet. Reportedly, she was told to lay her body on him and pinch him. The family does tend to make an effort to keep her from attending to the children. Priscilla, however, assumes primary care-taking responsibility for the children. Priscilla directs what goes on in terms of housekeeping, cooking, watching and feeding the children, and so on, and Valerie participates with verbal directions. Kevin has adapted to multiple caretakers. For example, if he asks Valerie for something and she does not reply favorably, he immediately goes to Priscilla. If she does not satisfy his needs, he then goes to Richard and then Mrs. James.

The family tends to speak in very loud tones to one another. The adults speak very loudly to the children in the form of reprimands and demands. The Families First social worker observed very little verbal bonding in the family.

It has also been observed that Valerie communicates with Keith as if he were an adult. For example, when Keith tried to reach for some fingernail polish, she said, "Don't do that! You know that's wrong! I don't want no funny bunny stuff! You know boys don't do that!"

Valerie, as well as the extended family, has limited knowledge regarding age-appropriate behaviors for children. On several occasions, the Families First social worker saw the family feed 7 month-old Keith pork steak, uncut ravioli, and large chunks of an apple. On one occasion, she observed Valerie giving the infant milk and asked why Keith was not receiving cereal in his milk. Valerie's response was, "I don't want him to be fat."

The family's eating patterns are very erratic, and the children are fed when and what the adults eat. Kevin was seen by the Families First social worker eating noodles at 9:00 a.m. and rice with his hands. Kevin has been seen serving himself and then going throughout the house eating. The Families First social worker has never observed a balanced meal being fed to the children (i.e., meat, vegetable, and starch at once).

Due to Kevin's erratic and unhealthy eating habits, the nurse and staff at Simpson Hospital state that he is having severe abdominal gas pains. The pains are causing him to walk humped over, and he frequently holds his abdomen.

Valerie does not acknowledge or accept responsibility for the abuse to Kevin. Valerie also reports not feeling responsible in any way for Kevin's behavior. She admits spanking Kevin, but she does not feel it was abuse. When questioned regarding her involvement or his environment being a factor in his behavior, Valerie responds by shutting down, becoming very defensive, or displaying inappropriate behaviors (yelling, avoiding eye contact, sarcastic comments, etc.). Valerie is not consistent in giving directions or setting rules for the children to follow. She often verbalizes that "I want them to obey and do what I tell them to do," but does not put plans in place to achieve this objective. Valerie has also commented that children should not be rewarded for things they are supposed to do. However, because of the inconsistencies of rules and inconsistency from child to child, the children in the home appear to be unsure as to what is required of them.

Valerie as well as some family members state that they want Kevin to come home from the hospital "normal." The Families First social worker discussed with Valerie the realities of medications' effect on behaviors, and having realistic versus unrealistic expectations. Valerie maintained that she was unsure whether she wanted Kevin to return home at all. On the other hand, she also advised that she would not work with the program if there was a chance that Keith would be taken from her.

Kevin

Kevin is a very active and talkative 6-year-old child, who will be going to first grade in the fall. It was recommended by his last teacher and the supervisor of the special education school district that Kevin attend a school for behaviorally disordered children. The recommendation was based on behaviors that were deemed unmanageable in the classroom—for example, self-mutilation, biting, scratching, pulling out hair, tearing clothes, stripping, and urinating on himself in front of the other students. Kevin also has some developmental issues. The same behaviors are said by Valerie to occur in the home. Valerie maintains that since the onset of Kevin's behavior problems at 3 years of age, they have escalated and become more severe. Valerie states that, in addition to the aforementioned behaviors, Kevin disrespects authority, curses, and threatens harm to others.

THE CEDENO FAMILY

Student Instructions

You are an intact family worker with a private child welfare agency. The Cedenos were referred to you by the Department of Children and Family Services (DCFS). Your agency's program goal is to work with families who have come to the attention of DCFS and provide family preservation interventions. DCFS will keep an open case on this family to ensure that they work with your agency. You are asked to make an analysis of the family situation and provide services to the family.

Family Composition

The Cedeno family is Mexican American and consists of the father, Benjamin, age 32, the mother, Nina, age 30, and their two children, Tamara, age 7, and their son, Sean, who is 3 years old. The Cedenos live in a two-story garden apartment. The apartment building appeared in need of repair.

Family Background

The Cedenos have been married for almost ten years. They met in Texas at a fiesta and have always been together. They have a family income of about $32,000 a year. They have not been able to save any money, because they have had to move four times in three years. Their parents were originally from Mexico. They are fluent in Spanish and abide by some of that culture's beliefs. Other Mexican families also live in the Cedenos' apartment complex. However, most of the Cedeno family resides in Texas. The Cedenos moved from Texas about three years ago to find better jobs.

Mrs. Cedeno has two sisters and three brothers, all of whom live in Texas. Her parents recently moved back to Mexico, and she does not see them much. Mr. Cedeno has five older brothers and three younger sisters. Most of his siblings live in Texas and California. He has one older brother and two younger sisters who live about 2 miles from him. He is very close to his family, but finances have prohibited him from returning to Texas or Mexico to visit other family members. The Cedenos hope to save enough money to move to Mexico.

Current Situation

A man called the child abuse hotline to report his concerns about a 3-year-old boy name Sean. He stated that he was Nina's co-worker. According to the reporter, Mrs. Cedeno confided in another co-worker that her husband "beat Sean with a belt last night." Several months ago, Mrs. Cedeno told another co-worker about her husband's "violent temper," but this is the first time she has said anything about her son being hurt. According to the reporter, Sean has come into the store twice with his mother with bruises on his face. On one occasion, Mrs. Cedeno said that her son was very clumsy and that he keeps falling off a swing at nursery school. The reporter told the hotline worker that he has reared three boys and that they rarely, if ever, got bruises on their faces, like those she saw on Sean. The reporter continued by noting that the Cedenos have a 7-year-old daughter, Tamara, and she seemed extremely shy. According to the reporter, Sean is enrolled at A New Beginning Child Development Center.

The Department of Children and Family Services (DCFS) Initial Involvement

The child protective services worker telephoned A New Beginning Child Development Center. The worker called the center to verify Sean's enrollment and spoke with Sylvia Greene, the director. Ms. Greene verified that

Sean was enrolled at the center and that he attends daily from 6:00 a.m. to 3:00 p.m.

The worker made a visit to A New Beginning Child Development Center. She met with Ms. Greene and Ms. Lee and observed Sean in the classroom. Ms. Lee said that Sean is "a lovable child, but he can be difficult." He has a very short attention span, he does not show much self-control, and he speaks very little English. Ms. Lee added, however, that Sean is not the only child in the class with these kinds of problems. Her main concern is that Sean is a "hitter" and a "biter." When Sean wants a toy that another child has, he hits or sometimes bites the child. The teacher feels that she has to watch Sean more closely than the other children to make sure that no one gets hurt. Ms. Lee stated that she told Sean's father last week that unless the biting stops, Sean will not be able to come to the center. Both Ms. Green and Ms. Lee say that the Cedenos are very cooperative parents and that Mrs. Cedeno is the active parent. They added that Mrs. Cedeno always drops Sean off in the morning and spends a few minutes with him before she leaves for work. Sean usually cries when she leaves.

The worker stated that her observation of Sean in the classroom revealed no unusual behaviors. Sean, a slender boy with brown eyes and dark brown hair, seemed quite happy. She did notice that he had difficulty sitting still for any length of time. He was neatly groomed and dressed. During his interactions with the other children he would speak Spanish. According to the teacher, nearly all the children get hurt on the playground occasionally, but that she was not aware of Sean ever falling off a swing hard enough to injure himself. The protective services worker examined Sean and found several bruises on his bottom. The marks appeared to be belt marks, and the skin was broken in two places. Sean would not tell her how he got the bruises; he just started crying and would not talk. The teacher appeared shocked and stated that she does not think that Sean is an "abused child." She told Ms. Greene that both parents seem very fond of him, and she does not remember ever seeing any injuries on Sean before, other than "normal kid bumps and bruises."

The worker then called the mother at work and asked her to come to the DCFS office. The mother was very concerned about the report and who made the report. She insisted that the children were okay and that they had no problems in the home. The worker advised the mother that she had gone to the school and had observed marks on Sean. Mrs. Cedeno agreed to come to the office and was asked to bring her husband. After about an hour Mrs. Cedeno came to the office with Sean and Tamara, but her husband was not with them. She said that her husband could not leave his job. She also stated to the worker that she would rather try and resolve the situation before her husband got involved. She appeared very nervous and stated that she thinks Sean got a little spanking last night for something, but she did not appear to remember what the spanking was for. She also stated that she had to work last night and was not at home. She attempted to ask Sean what happened, but he did not say anything. Mrs. Cedeno stated that Sean was not being abused and that she was sure that "if my husband whipped him, he has a good explanation." Tamara then spoke up and ran to her mother and said, "Mommy, Poppy hit Sean because Sean was being bad." Tamara started to cry and told her mother that she was afraid. Mrs. Cedeno hugged her children and assured them that everything was going to be okay. Mrs. Cedeno started that the worker was welcome to come to their home to talk to Mr. Cedeno.

The worker went to the Cedeno home. Mrs. Cedeno answered the door. She said Mr. Cedeno was just getting up and would join them soon. Mrs. Cedeno looked very tired and tense. She is an attractive woman with dark brown hair and light brown eyes—just like Sean. The apartment was in disarray.

While waiting for Mr. Cedeno, Mrs. Cedeno said her husband was very angry about the report on Sean. She said her husband had expected a promotion to store manager but had not gotten it and that "he has been upset for two weeks and now this." Mr. Cedeno is a tall, middle-built man with curly hair. When he walked into the room, he immediately asked Mrs. Cedeno in Spanish to go fix him a cup of coffee. Then he asked the worker angrily, "Now what's this all about?" The report was explained. Mr. Cedeno interrupted and said that Sean always has bruises on him from one fall after another. "Sean is a nightmare." (Mrs. Cedeno sat quietly and looked out the window.) Mr. Cedeno was asked to explain what he meant by "nightmare." He said that Sean never listens to his mother and that he only listens to him (Mr. Cedeno) when he threatens him with the belt. Mr. Cedeno continued by relating a series of incidents in which Sean misbehaved. For example, Sean breaks his toys as soon as he gets them, and he throws objects when he is frustrated. A few weeks ago, Sean threw a metal truck and hit Tamara in the head, causing her to need five stitches. Mr. Cedeno said, "I was so mad I saw black. I didn't allow Sean to play outside for two weeks. He stayed in his room most of the time." When kept in his room last week for wetting the bed, Sean threw his toys everywhere, tore up several books, and even ripped the window shades down onto the floor. Both parents seemed relieved to hear that Sean was behaving well at school today. Mrs. Cedeno said that she was unaware of Sean ever biting another child at school or anywhere else, and she would talk to Ms. Lee about "the problem" tomorrow.

The worker encouraged the Cedenos to talk more about Sean. Mrs. Cedeno was more tolerant of Sean's "active behavior" than Mr. Cedeno. She said she never "laid a hand" on either of her children. In response, Mr. Cedeno said rather sarcastically, "And that's why Sean acts the way he does."

Because of the Cedenos work schedules, the family rarely has any meals or leisure time together. Mrs. Cedeno always gets the children to and from school. Tamara makes breakfast for herself and Sean, which, according to Mrs. Cedeno, "is a big help." Mr. Cedeno frequently works on weekends. Again, rather sarcastically, he added, "My wife has bankers' hours." In response, Mrs. Cedeno glared at her husband, but said nothing.

Sean

According to Mrs. Cedeno, Sean is able to entertain himself. He likes to build with blocks, knock the blocks down, and build again; and he likes to watch TV, especially *Barney*. He and Tamara usually get along reasonably well. Mrs. Cedeno also said that Sean is an affectionate child and that he likes her to sit and hold him and tell him stories—an activity she, unfortunately, has little time for. Mr. Cedeno stated that "Sean has his mother wrapped around his little finger." The worker asked them how they typically discipline the children. Mr. Cedeno said he believes "children need a good whipping now and then." He acknowledged that he physically spanks Sean and Tamara but never hard enough to hurt them or leave bruises. He states he rarely has to discipline Tamara.

Tamara

Tamara is an attractive child, but she appears tired. She has dark circles under her eyes. Tamara is friendly but reserved. She is a smart child academically, and is obedient. Tamara enjoys listening to tapes and learning to read. According to her mother, Tamara does not like to watch television.

SAFETY AND RISK ASSESSMENT QUESTIONS

1. What form of physical abuse is present in this family?

2. What are the specific injuries to the child or children?

3. How do these injuries guide intervention?

4. How does the abuse impact protection of the child or other children in the home?

5. Does the abuse impact family preservation? Explain.

6. What cultural factors must be considered in the determination of what constitutes physical abuse in this family?

7. How do these factors impact your perception or ability to work with this family?

FAMILY CASE ANALYSIS—ENGAGEMENT

1. What is the presenting problem? How are the family members involved in the situation defining the problem?

2. In exploring the situation, how does the information that you learn from other family members inform your perceptions?

3. How would you define the working problem based on the current information?

4. What strategies do you think would be useful in engaging with the individuals involved?

FAMILY ASSESSMENT

1. How would your definition of the working problem direct your assessment?

2. What assumptions about human and social behavior are you making, and how would you follow up with these?

3. Are there other problems or issues you think might emerge as you delve deeper into this case? What are they, and how might they affect the situation?

4. What information are you lacking about the situation and its context that you feel you need to know to gain an in-depth understanding?

5. Identify the strengths, limitations, and barriers present in this family. Based on the strengths, where would you start to work with this family?

6. What issues of motivation and/or resistance do you think you are likely to encounter? How do you think you might handle them?

7. Give a clear and concise summary of your assessment and state how it affects the defining of general goals.

8. Identify and briefly state at least two theoretical frameworks or approaches that would guide your intervention in working with this family.

9. Prepare a genogram and an ecomap for the family, using the blanks given as Figures 2.1 and 2.2.

The _____ Family

Male   ▶ Pregnancy   – – – Marital separation   ? Whereabouts unknown

○ Female   ×× Death   ⋯/⋯ Divorce

FIGURE 2.1   The Family Genogram
(Sketch a genogram of the facts of this family structure.)

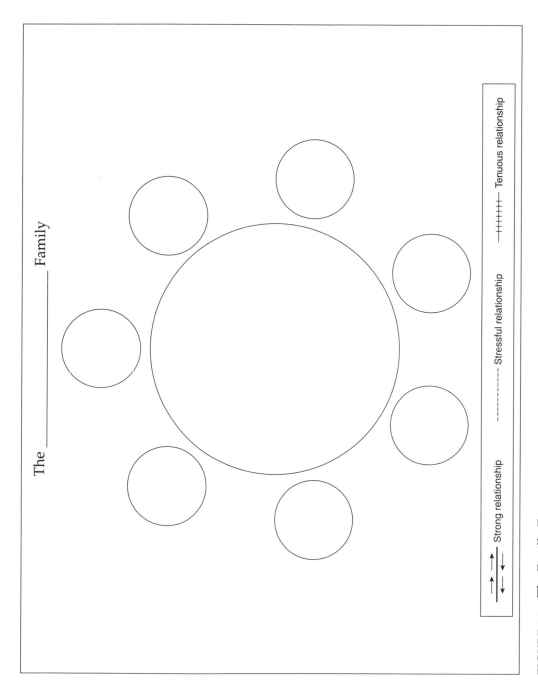

The _____ Family

Strong relationship   Stressful relationship   Tenuous relationship

FIGURE 2.2   The Family Ecomap

PLANNING FOR THE FAMILY

1. State your general goals in working with this family.

2. State specific objectives related to each goal and identify specific changes in the situation that might lead to accomplishing the above goals.

3. What actions should be taken by the worker, the clients, or others to operationalize your objectives?

4. How are you going to set up your evaluation to track accomplishments or progress in goals and objectives? (*Note:* This section should reflect knowledge of methods of practice evaluation.)

FAMILY TREATMENT PLAN/CONTRACT

Design a treatment plan for this family. This is an example of a treatment/contract plan. Most practice texts provide examples.

The Brown Family Treatment/Contract Plan

Client: _____ (Define the client here.)

I. **Brief Description of the Problem**
(This is generally a summary of the reasons the client came to you or your agency.)

II. **Primary Goals and Objectives** (Find a format that is clear to your client and you.)
    1. Goal:

        Objective:

    2. Goal:

        Objective:

    3. Goal:

        Objective:

III. We, the undersigned, agree to the following tasks:

  1.

  2.

IV. Evaluation of Progress (How your plan will be evaluated.)

_____

_____   Signature of Social Worker

_____

Signature(s) of Client(s)

_____   _____

(Date)   (Date)

SUGGESTED READINGS

Alexander, P. C., Moore, S., & Alexander, E. R. III. (1991). What is transmitted in the intergenerational transmission of violence? *Journal of Marriage and Family, 53,* 657–668.

Allen, M. (1992). *Redefining Family Reunification.* Iowa City, IA: National Resource Center on Family Based Services.

Altshuler, S. J., & Gleeson, J. P. (1999). Completing the evaluation triangle for the next century: Measuring child "well-being" in family foster care. *Child Welfare, 28,* 125–147.

Brissett-Chapman, S. (1997). Child protection risk assessment and African American children: Cultural ramification for families and communities. *Child Welfare, 76(1),* 45–63.

Buriel, R., Loya, T., Gonda, T., & Klessen, K. (1979). Child abuse and neglect referral patterns of Angelo and Mexican Americans. *Hispanic Journal of Behavioral Sciences, 1,* 215–227.

Combs-Orme, T., & Thomas, K. H. (1997). Assessment of troubled families. *Social Work Research, 21(4),* 261–269.

Douglass, A. (1996). Rethinking the effects of homelessness on children: Resiliency and competency. *Child Welfare, 75(6),* 741–751.

Easterlin, R. A. (1982). The changing circumstances of child-rearing. *Journal of Communication, 32,* 86–98.

Ferguson, H. (1997). Protecting children in new times: Child protection and the risk society. *Child and Family Social Work, 2(4),* 221–234.

Gardner, H. (1996). The concept of family: Perceptions of children in family foster care. *Child Welfare, 75(2),* 161–182.

Giovanni, J. M. (1995). Reports of child maltreatment from mandated and non-mandated reporters. *Children and Youth Services Review, 17(4),* 487–501.

Grubbs, G. A. (1994). An abused child's use of sandplay in the healing process. *Social Work Journal, 22(2),* 193–209.

Herman, K. C. (1995). Appropriate use of the Child Abuse Potential Inventory in a Big Brothers/Big Sisters agency. *Journal of Social Service Research, 20(3/4),* 93–103.

Hough, K. J., & Erwin, P. G. (1997) Children's attitudes toward violence on television. *The Journal of Psychology, 131*(4), 411–415.

Hurst, N. C., & Sawatzky, D. D. (1996). Families with multiple problems through a bowenian lens. *Child Welfare, 75*(6), 693–708.

Keller, J., & McDade, K. (1997). Cultural diversity and help-seeking behavior: Sources of help and obstacles to support for parents. *Journal of Multicultural Social Work, 5*(1/2), 63–78.

Lawrence-Webb, C. (1997). African American children in the modern child welfare system: a legacy of the Flemming rule. *Child Welfare, 76*(1), 9–30.

Lenton, R. (1995, July). Power versus feminist theories of wife abuse. Special issue: Focus on the Violence Against Women Survey. *Canadian Journal of Criminology, 37*(3), 305–330.

Loos, M. E., & Alexander, P. C. (1997, June). Differential effects associated with self-reported histories of abuse and neglect. *Journal of Interpersonal Violence, 12*(3), 340–360.

Markward, M. J. (1997). The impact of domestic violence on children. *Families in Society, 78*(1), 66–70.

McNeal, C., & Amato, P. R. (1998, March). Parents marital violence long-term consequences for children. *Journal of Family Issues, 19*(2), 123–139.

McPhatter, A. R. (1997). Cultural competence in child welfare: What is it? How do we achieve it? What happens without it? *Child Welfare, 76*(1), 255–278.

Owusu-Bempah, J., & Howitt, D. (1997). Sociogenealogical connectedness, attachment theory, and childcare practice. *Children and Family Social Work, 2*(4), 199–207.

Peltoniemi, T. (1985). Child abuse and physical punishment of children in Finland. *Child Abuse and Neglect, 7*, 33–36.

Roys, P. (1989). Ethnic minorities in the child welfare system. *International Journal of Child Psychiatry, 30*, 102–118.

Smith, S. L., Sullivan, Q. E., & Cohen, A. H. (1995). Factors associated with the indication of child abuse reports. *Journal of Social Service Research, 21*(1), 15–34.

Smithey, M. (1997). Infant homicide at the hands of mothers: Toward a sociological perspective. *Deviant Behavior, 18*(3), 255–272.

Solheim, J. S. (1982). A cross-cultural comparison of the use of corporal punishment on children: A focus on the United States and Sweden. *Child Abuse and Neglect, 6*, 147–154.

Wells, S. K., & Fluke, J. D. (1995). The decision to investigate: Child protective practice in twelve local agencies. *Children and Youth Services Review, 17*(4): 523–546.

CHAPTER THREE

NEGLECT
Physical, Medical, Educational

THE HENDERSON FAMILY

Student Instructions

You have just been assigned to investigate allegations of medical neglect of Sally Ann, made by her maternal aunt, Sue Ann Martin. Mrs. Martin states that she received a call from her nephew, David, stating that his sister, Sally Ann, has a swollen eye and that their parents will not take her to the doctor. Mrs. Martin states that she spoke to her sister and her sister told her to "mind her own business." She is concerned and wants someone to get some help for her niece.

Family Composition

The Henderson family consists of the parents, Albert, age 39, and Lisa Ann, age 40. They have three children, a son, David, age 17, and two daughters, Sally Ann, age 12, and Elizabeth, age 9. The extended family that is involved in this situation are a maternal aunt, Sue Ann Martin, age 35, and a paternal aunt, Carolyn Henderson-Smith, age 34.

Current Situation

Sally Ann woke up about three weeks ago with a swollen eye. She showed her mother and her mother told her to put a cold towel on it and lay down. The mother told her to pray for her healing. Nothing has changed in more than two weeks. Mrs. Henderson is refusing to take Sally Ann to the doctor, because she does not believe in modern medicine—it conflicts with her religious beliefs. About a week ago, the maternal aunt went to see Sally Ann at home and her eye was swollen shut. Sally Ann has not been to school in almost two weeks. The school is concerned, but Mrs. Henderson told the teacher that Sally Ann is getting better and will be back to school next week.

The Hendersons believe that God will heal Sally Ann. They are Christian Scientists. Mr. Henderson has told his wife that Sally Ann's eye seems to be getting worse and he thinks he needs to treat it or have her eyes seen by a doctor; however, his wife reminded him that he needed to have more faith. Mrs. Henderson feels that Sally Ann's eye will not heal because of a lack of faith of the people around her. The Hendersons usually isolate themselves when someone in the family is sick. The Hendersons are firm believers of their faith.

Family Background

Albert and Lisa Ann Henderson are a Caucasian couple who have been married for nineteen years. They reside in an upper-middle-class neighborhood. Albert and Lisa met in college and fell in love. Lisa Ann got her degree in chemistry and considers herself a person who loves science. Albert was a pre-med major in college, and while doing his residency as a physician, he was always concerned about the "sicknesses of the world." He was very committed to his job as a physician. However, recently he decided to leave medicine and pursue another career.

About twelve years ago, Lisa Ann started to study Christian Science. She was introduced to this perspective by one of her older brothers. She is very committed to the religion. About five years ago, Albert agreed to join the faith, because he states he has seen so many doctors make major mistakes and people die at the hands of doctors. He thinks if people could have faith in God they could be healed. Both Lisa and Albert were raised as Catholics. They feel that as Christian Scientists they have developed a stronger faith.

Lisa Ann has four other siblings, two older brothers, one younger brother, and one younger sister. They were very close as children, but in the last five years Mrs. Henderson has become estranged from her family. Her two older brothers are Christian Scientists. They used to study the doctrine together. However, recently she has not even spoken to them. Her parents are very concerned about her, but they live about twenty-five hours away and are not very close to Lisa Ann or her family.

Albert has only one sister, with whom he is very close. However, she does not interfere in his life when it comes to religion. He states that his sister respects his decision to worship whatever religion he chooses. He feels fairly strongly about his faith; this is the first time he has felt ambivalent about their decision not to have Sally Ann seen by the doctor. He went into medicine because both of his parents had terminal illnesses and he always wanted to know how to heal people. He has told his wife that if Sally Ann's eye does not get any better in the next few days, he will take her to a doctor. As a result, his wife is very angry with him and he cannot seem to communicate with her anymore. According to him, she has literally stopped communicating with everyone. He is very concerned about his children. He says this situation with Sally Ann's eye has really shed a lot of light on their family situation.

David

David is the oldest child. He is 17 years old and is very independent. He is beginning to question the validity of their faith. He thinks his parents are being unrealistic and that they need to have open minds. He feels frustrated because his best friend's father is a medical doctor and he has been discussing his religious beliefs with him. David is becoming more defiant toward his parents because he says they will not listen although he has tried to talk to them. Recently, when he attempted to talk to his parents, his mother made him stay home from school and together they read about the history and doctrine of Christian Science. He would like to go and live with his aunt, Sue Ann, but his mother says definitely not. David attempted to talk to his father and his father tried to listen, but told him that maybe his faith is just being challenged now. His father also told him that his mother would be angry to learn that they were having this conversation. David is contemplating running away because he has become so angry at his parents, especially his mother.

Sally Ann

Sally Ann is a very obedient child. She is friendly and has a strong faith. She loves being a Christian Scientist and finds the whole idea of having faith very exciting. She attends the youth group at church and is always telling her friends at school about her religion. She also knows that she gets a lot of attention from her mother by being a "true believer." Her mother brags about her and tells her how proud she is of her. Sally Ann is a good student but not an A student. She has been somewhat sickly. When she was first born, her parents had only been Christian Scientists for about six months. Sally Ann had her initial immunizations, but her parents have not taken her to a doctor since she was a baby. Sally Ann is concerned about her eye, but thinks it is not healing because one day she felt she doubted her faith by telling her friend at school that she wished her mother would take her to the doctor to get medicine. Sally Ann is concerned that she will get behind in her school work because she has missed so much school. Sally Ann will not question her parents' decision because she does not want her parents to be angry and she knows they have to deal with David. However, Sally Ann is becoming afraid because her eye really hurts and she is really praying hard and nothing seems to be happening.

Elizabeth

Elizabeth is the youngest child. She is 9 years old and also very involved in the youth program at the Christian Science church. She does not really understand the doctrine but is excited about participating in the programs because she has made a lot of friends in them. When she was a baby, her aunt, Sue Ann, babysat her while her parents worked. Sue Ann took her to the doctor and got her all of her immunizations. Elizabeth is a very healthy girl and very friendly. She is somewhat confused about what she hears at school and what she is taught at home. But she does not worry about it because she has her friends at school.

Extended Family

Sue Ann Martin is Mrs. Henderson's sister. Sue Ann states that she is concerned about the health and welfare of her sister's children. She is most concerned about her niece Sally Ann's eye and is afraid she might lose her eyesight if she does not see a doctor. Sue Ann states that she remembers when all of the children were sick with the flu. They were throwing up, but her sister and her husband refused to give the children any medicines. Sue Ann states that the children were sick for about two months and the parents just prayed for their healing. Sue Ann states although the children got better, it took them too long to get well. Sue Ann says that she is afraid for them because when the children are sick, the parents isolate them from everyone. Sue Ann says she got a call from David telling her about the situation and asking her to do something about Sally Ann's eye.

THE PEREZ FAMILY

Student Instructions

You are working as a protective services case worker in the local state child welfare agency. You have been assigned to investigate the Perez family for possible educational neglect. The family is Puerto Rican, and their primary language is Spanish. They speak very little English. You do not speak Spanish, and you know little about Puerto Rican culture. You will have to meet with the family and a case worker from the Educational Alternative Center within seventy-two hours. However, because of the language barrier, you are feeling overwhelmed with this case. You also wonder if this family is getting pushed around by the system because they are unable to communicate their needs. You have asked your supervisor to assign the case to someone else, but there is no one in your office who speaks Spanish. The Juvenile Court Probations Department has requested a social history and a recommendation from you in one week.

Family Composition

The Perez family consists of the primary caretakers, Carlos, age 59, and Melinda, age 56, who are the grandparents. They have two grandchildren, Raphael, Jr., age 15, and Maritza, age 7. The father, Raphael, Sr., age 35, is in and out of the home. The mother, Martha, age 31, no longer resides in the home but is involved in the children's lives.The maternal grandmother, Calina Ruiz, age 52, is also involved in the family.

Current Situation

Raphael is a 15-year-old male and in the tenth grade. He was referred to the Smith County Juvenile Court for chronic truancy. At the time of the referral, Raphael was attending Smith High School. Smith High School is located in a predominately white community. There are a few minority families, all of whom live outside the city limits. Raphael refuses to attend, and when he is brought to school, he runs away. Raphael was referred to juvenile court because he had missed six consecutive weeks of school. When the probation officer was unable to get any information, the case was referred to the Department of Children and Family Services. According to the public school social work staff, they first noticed problems in Raphael's behavior about a year ago. They did not think much about it because the teacher had reported that she heard that "during harvest seasons many Mexican children cannot go to school, because they have to work." The Juvenile Court referred him to the Educational Alternative Center for students who are truant and on the verge of being kicked out of the public school system. He has been attending the Educational Alternative Center for approximately a week, but has already missed two days. The probation officer has taken a special interest in this child and believes that something else is going on in his family.

Family Background

Raphael's parents separated when he was 8. His mother, Martha, moved to another city, leaving him and his sister with their father. She continues to reside in a different city than the children. After the separation, Raphael's father moved them to a small rural town where he could get work. When Raphael was 9, his father left the home. This time Raphael and his sister were left in the care of their paternal grandparents, who speak very little English. On occasion, his father would come around to make sure they were all doing okay. Raphael speaks both English and Spanish well. His grandparents depend on him to translate for them. Raphael is experiencing some emotional problems, and his behavior has changed drastically from what it was a year ago. Raphael was recently diagnosed with depression by the local mental health center and has been put on medication. His grandparents are afraid because he does not communicate with them anymore. He just sits and stares out of the window.

His grandparents have told Raphael, "no more school" and "no more medicine." When the school social worker went to the home she was told that Raphael was sick; however, some neighbors have called the school and stated that they see him shopping in town and attending to family business. The school social worker attempted to speak to the grandparents and they said "no entiendo," meaning they did not understand. According to the school social worker, Raphael's grandfather does not speak any English and has a drinking problem, and his grandmother can speak only a little English. The school social worker stated that Raphael's grandparents came to the United States about eight years ago and are working as migrant workers.

Raphael Perez, Sr.

Raphael, Sr., is 35 years old. He has eight siblings, two brothers who reside in the United States and six sisters who reside in Puerto Rico. He finished high school and went to college for two years before coming to the United States. He has battled with alcohol since he was 20 years old, but is now a recovering alcoholic. He has been arrested three times for driving while intoxicated. Each time he was coming from work.

Approximately ten years ago, Raphael, Sr., and his wife, Martha, came to the United States and brought Raphael, Jr., with them. Raphael, Sr., worked three jobs so that he could bring his parents to the States as well. According to Raphael, Jr., his father started drinking heavily about five years ago, but stopped about a year ago and has been sober since that time. About a month ago, he disappeared for four days and no one knew his whereabouts. When he returned home, he had no money and had been drinking. He has lost two of his jobs, and they do not have another source of stable income. He loves his children but feels they are better off with his parents. He has been thinking lately that maybe he should send the family back to Puerto Rico because they do not have enough family in this country to support them.

Martha Perez

Martha, Raphael's mother, is 31 years old. She has three siblings, one brother and two sisters. Martha recently got her GED and states that she has a good job. Since she left the home, she has not supported the children either financially or emotionally. According to Raphael, she works at night, but he does not know what she does. His father has told him that his mother is a prostitute and that she uses drugs. Raphael and his sister visited their mother about six months ago and he stated that they had a good visit but had to return home because there was no one with his grandparents. Martha is not sure she wants the children to come and live with her. She states that she hardly knows Maritza and that Raphael is needed by his grandparents, because they do not have any friends or family who can help them get around. Also, she is afraid that if she takes the children back, her husband will want to come back, and she does not think that she could live with him again. She says that on two occasions when her husband was drinking he became violent and struck her in the face, and that is what made her leave him. Martha states that her father is deceased now, but she remembers her father drinking and beating her mother whenever he felt like it, and she saw the same thing happening to her. She decided to get out of the situation even if she had to leave her children. She remembers being angry at her mother for allowing her father to beat her. She says her mother appeared relieved when her father died. She further states that her mother currently lives with one of her sisters and her sister's three children. Martha says that she has a lot of support because they live only about a mile from her.

Raphael, Jr.

Raphael, Jr., is a 15-year-old boy who has had to grow up very quickly. He used to be an above-average student. He loved school, and he had become quite popular at his school as a Spanish tutor. He was well liked by his peers. He has always been a very responsible young man. He is very respectful to his parents and grandparents. Raphael is quiet and often does not speak up when he disagrees with something. However, recently he told his grandparents that he is very disappointed in his father, although he loves him very much. For the last three months Raphael has been very depressed about their situation and he does not know what to do. Raphael wants to go to school, participate in after-school activities, and go to school dances, but he is afraid to leave his grandparents alone. He feels guilty about having fun sometimes. He also feels that he has to care for Maritza.

Maritza

Maritza is 7 years old and in the second grade at the local elementary school. Maritza is very smart and shy, but a happy, healthy child. She is bilingual, but enjoys speaking Spanish more than English. She has not bonded with her mother or father, because she has been raised by her grandparents and Raphael. She calls her grandparents "Mommy" and "Poppy." She is very close to Raphael, who takes her to school every day and picks her up.

THE BERNARDEZ FAMILY

Student Instructions

You are working as a family preservation worker with the Department of Children and Family Services (DCFS). You have been assigned to work with the Bernardez family. The department recently started a new program to work with families dealing with substance abuse. The purpose of this program is to work with families in which substance abuse is the primary problem. The parents have voluntarily agreed to work with your program as an alternative to having their children removed from the home. They have been arrested for possession of marijuana and for domestic violence. They asked the judge to give them a chance to keep their family together. The judge placed both parents on probation, contingent upon them getting drug treatment, marital counseling for domestic violence, and working with your program. If they fail to get treatment and complete your program, they will go to jail and possibly lose their children. You will meet them on Friday. They have completed one week of treatment.

Family Composition

The Bernardez family consists of the parents, Felix, age 35, and Marisa, age 30. They have two daughters, Danielle, age 9, and Nicole, age 7. The paternal grandmother, Lena Bernardez, and the maternal grandparents, Jose and Helena Messina, are involved with the family. They do not reside in the home. The family is from Guatemala.

Current Situation

Mr. and Mrs. Bernardez started smoking marijuana together about five years ago. About six months ago, Mrs. Bernardez went out with a few friends and experimented with crack cocaine and found she liked it. About two months ago Mr.Bernardez found out that she was using crack, and he is very angry. As a result, they do not smoke together anymore. He has asked her to stop using drugs altogether. She is refusing to stop, and Mr. Bernardez feels that their marriage is in trouble. He states that she cannot handle crack, because he has come home on two occasions and found their two children dirty and hungry. He has asked her to get some help or leave the house. Mr. Bernardez stated that he came home one evening and found Mrs. Bernardez doing drugs in front of the children. He states that he was so angry that they started to fight. Their oldest daughter, Danielle, age 9, took her sister, Nicole, age 7, and ran across the street to a neighbor's house. The neighbor called their paternal grandmother, who lives only a block away; she came and picked up the children and then called the police.

The police took both parents to jail. At their bond hearing, the judge told them to either go to treatment and try and get their family back together or go to jail. They agreed to go to treatment. Mr. Bernardez called his mother, and she agreed to keep the children while they are in treatment. She has agreed to keep them for a little while, but no one knows how long they might have to stay in treatment. During the intake interview, the counselor advised them that she will have to make a referral to DCFS. They are very angry because they did not want anyone to find out about this. They fear they will lose their jobs and everything they have worked so hard for.

Family Background

The Bernardez family is a lower-middle-class family living in a working-class neighborhood. Their annual income is about $60,000 a year. The parents are originally from Guatemala, but they have raised their children in the United States. Both parents acknowledged their difficulty in fitting into this country when they first moved here. They started using drugs to make friends with people at Mr. Bernardez's job.

Felix Bernardez

Mr. Bernardez is employed with a major firm as a computer operator. He has been having problems on the job for several years, as his new boss has problems with people who speak another language. He has used drugs socially on special occasions, but never felt he was addicted. He has been on this job for eight years and thought this job was a "gift from heaven." He does not see himself as an addict, but says that he often wishes he could stop using drugs, because he knows that it is not good and he is not setting a good example for his children. He has a good reputation at his job and does not want anyone to know what is going on. However, he only has two weeks vacation, and everyone at his job thinks he is on vacation. He does not know what he will do about the next two weeks or if he will have to leave treatment. He does not want to leave because he does not want to lose his children or go to jail.

Marisa Bernardez

Mrs. Bernardez is also working. She is an elementary Spanish teacher in the local public school. She has also used drugs with her husband socially. However, in the last six months she has tried crack occasionally and is finding that she likes it. Mr. Bernardez is upset, as he thinks she is addicted. She disagrees, and this is causing marital problems. She states that it is not affecting her job yet, but she is in charge of the "say no to drugs" program at the school. She feels guilty for using, but feels that she can stop any time she wants. She is very emotionally upset, as she cannot believe that she and Mr. Bernardez had a fight and that their children saw it. She has called her school and asked to take two weeks of sick leave. She must bring a doctor's note to the principal when she returns. She does not know what to do, and she fears that if the school board finds out they will fire her. She is disappointed in herself, as she feels a lot of kids look up to her in the school because of the "say no to drugs" program.

Danielle

Danielle is 9 years old, and a very intelligent child. She is an A student and attends the same school at which her mother works. She speaks Spanish and English fluently and is well liked by her teacher. Her teacher has recently noticed a change in her behavior and is wondering what is wrong with her. Danielle wants to tell her teacher what she saw at home and that her parents are in a drug program, but she is afraid to say anything, as her grandmother told her not to say anything to anybody because her family will be in trouble. Danielle is becoming very sad because of her home life. She does not play with her friends at school and is becoming more withdrawn every day. She has a best friend and thinks she can share the secret with her, but is too afraid.

Nicole

Nicole is 7 years old and usually very friendly. However, lately she is often sad and appears distracted. She used to laugh all the time. She attends private school, because her parents thought she might need more attention. Nicole is not as bright as Danielle. Nicole is into playing with Barbie dolls, and she speaks little Spanish. She does not know specifically what is going on in the family. Recently, she has been creating more imaginary friends and is beginning to talk about those friends at school, and the teacher is accusing her of lying. Also, she is in a Brownie troop and they do a lot of activities. Nicole is close to her Brownie leader and has been asking to spend the night with her on a weekly basis. The Brownie leader has talked to the parents and the parents state that Nicole is just infatuated with the leader because of the fun she has with her. After observing the domestic dispute between her parents, Nicole has become more withdrawn and sad. She is close to her father, but lately she does not even talk to him or allow him to hug her.

Extended Family

Lena Bernardez is the paternal grandmother with whom the children are currently staying. She is from Guatemala and has been in the United States for only seven years. She came to the United States after her husband died. Felix is her only son; she has two older daughters, one in New York and the other in Guatemala. She speaks both English and Spanish, but mostly Spanish. Her English is not as good as she would like it to be. She describes herself as a Christian woman and is totally against any kind of "wrong-doings." She often comments to her son about how bad drugs are in Guatemala and that she is so glad that she and her children never used drugs. She lives on her own in a small senior citizens' apartment complex nearby. She often babysits the girls when the parents have to go out. However, she cannot keep the girls for long, because of the rules of the building—only the person whose name is on the lease can live there. Others can come to visit, but not for more than thirty days. She loves her son and his family and is very upset, as she was not aware that they were using drugs. She is always bragging to her friends and family in Guatemala about how successful they are. Her grandchildren love her very much.

Helena and Jose Messina are the maternal grandparents. They live in a city nearby that is approximately three hours' drive from the Bernardez's. They have four children, two older boys and a daughter younger than Marisa. They too are from Guatemala and are a very proud Latino family. Marisa called them to come and get the children. When they arrived, they demanded to know what was going on. Lena told them everything. They have been very supportive of the family, but they are very angry about this situation. They are disappointed in Mr. Bernardez, and they feel it is all his fault. Mr. Messina said, "What kind of man would allow his wife to use drugs?" Mr. Messina says that he is so angry with them that he does not know what to do. They had a very good relationship with Mr. Bernardez up until now. Mr. Messina has often told Felix how much he respects him and appreciates his taking care of his daughter and grandchildren.

THE PHILLIPS FAMILY

Student Instructions

You are employed as a social worker with the Society for Children. Your agency's primary focus is family preservation. You have been assigned to work with the Phillips family. The family was referred to your agency by the Department of Children and Family Services (DCFS) for family preservation services. The family has been served by other social service agencies, but after a review of the case the committee felt that this family needed more one-on-one direct services. An assessment of the current family situation is needed.

Family Composition

The Phillips family consists of the mother, Keisha, age 22, and her three children. She has one son, Jeremy, age 4, and two daughters, KeKe, age 7, and Alexia, age 15 months. The family resides in the Third Chance Shelter for families. Ms. Phillips reported that before first coming to a shelter, she and her family had been living with her aunt, Erline Phillips, in Jackson, Mississippi. She suggested that her aunt has played many roles in her life, and said that her Aunt Erline was the person who raised her.

Current Situation

The Department of Children and Family Services referred Ms. Keisha Phillips to your agency after her case was substantiated for inadequate shelter and inadequate supervision of her children. Ms. Phillips and her three children were residing at the Holy Sisters Shelter. However, the case worker at the shelter requested that Ms. Phillips and her children move out, after repeated warnings to supervise the children appropriately. Reports from the shelter staff noted that Ms. Phillips would be upstairs while the children were downstairs (or vice versa), and she was unable to keep her 4-year-old son, Jeremy, from leaning out the second-floor window. After Ms. Phillips was asked to leave, no shelter was available to accommodate her and her children. She placed an application at the Good Samaritan homeless shelter, but she was told that there would be no openings for six months. However, Third Chance Shelter was able to accommodate her and her children, though under very strict rules. Ms. Phillips agreed to the rules of the shelter. She has been there only two weeks, but the shelter has repeatedly discussed consequences with her and informed her that if the problem of supervision of her children continues they will give her seventy-two hours to vacate.

According to the social worker, the communication patterns between Ms. Phillips and her children are nontraditional. For example, she talks to her children as though they are adults. She is not affectionate or nurturing with any of the children, although she will hold them to stop them from crying. Ms. Phillips believes that the only way the children will listen to her is if she spanks or punishes them. She feels the "no hitting" rule at the shelter is causing problems with disciplining the children, and that the children refuse to obey her because they are aware that she cannot hit them, and therefore they tend to push her to the limit. She wants to get out of the shelter so that she can regain control over her children.

Family Background

The Phillips family is not new to DCFS. There are previous substantiated child abuse and neglect reports in regard to the children. Other reports include the fact that Ms. Phillip's uncle, Cecil Phillips, was arrested for sexually abusing Ms. Phillips' oldest daughter, KeKe, who is now 7 years old. Also, Ms. Phillips' grandmother was arrested a year ago for physically abusing all of Ms. Phillips' children. All of the children sustained severe cuts, welts, and bruises all over their bodies. Ms. Phillips was advised not to leave her children with her mother. No other services were recommended to the family at that time.

During the intake interview on this current situation, Ms. Phillips reported using marijuana approximately three to four times a week and crack cocaine on occasion. The investigator referred her to an outpatient recovery center for a substance abuse assessment. However, she did not keep the appointment.

Ms. Phillips has no income, due to her inability to comply with the Department of Human Services. This is her third reported sanction, and she has not received cash assistance in two years. She is expected to comply with the child support division and obtain her GED in order to have her cash assistance reinstated. Ms. Phillips' public assistance case worker has informed the agency that until she complies with the rules, she cannot qualify for housing or cash assistance. Ms. Phillips has been told that she will also need to find employment for TANF (Temporary Assistance for Needy Families) to continue with cash assistance when this is reinstated.

In addition, all of Ms. Phillips' case workers and social workers have concerns about her continued inability to provide appropriate supervision of her three children. Ms. Phillips was asked to leave the first shelter (Holy Sisters), because of her repeated failure to ensure supervision of her 4-year-old son, Jeremy. Since she moved to the Third Chance Shelter, the case worker has had consistent reports from the staff and residents regarding the same problem of lack of supervision. On one occasion while at Third Chance Shelter, her oldest daughter, KeKe, fell and needed fifteen stitches to the top of her lip. The social worker at Third Chance has discussed appropriate supervision plans with Ms. Phillips numerous times. The shelter has repeatedly discussed consequences with the client and has informed her that should the problem continue, they would give her seventy-two hours to vacate. To compound the issue of inadequate supervision, the social worker has discussed with Ms. Phillips the need to meet for individual counseling at least three times a week. The social worker is also concerned about the overwhelming history of incest in this family. Ms. Phillips has indicated that her father sexually abused her from age 7 until age 14. However, there is no record with DCFS of a call to the hotline or any intervention on Ms. Phillips' behalf. Just recently, she revealed that her paternal uncle sexually abused her as well.

Ms. Phillips has also indicated that she was sexually abused by other family members. She also told the social worker that she would not want her to know who KeKe's father is. When the social worker asked her why not, she said that she did not want to discuss it. The social worker asked Mrs. Phillips if it was a family member, and she said "yes" but would not identify the person. KeKe was also sexually assaulted for two years by her uncle, Cedric Phillips (a registered sex offender, according to Ms. Phillips), and the social worker has reason to believe that Jeremy may have been subjected to sexual abuse as well, given his behaviors.

Ms. Phillips states that all three of her children have different fathers and she is not aware of where any of them live. Jeremy's father's name is Melvin Wilson and is believed to live somewhere in Detroit, Michigan. Keisha has not been able to contact him. Mason Farmer, who is Alexia's father, lives and works in eastern Michigan. Holy Sisters Shelter reports state that Mr. Farmer has come to the shelter and picked Alexia up and kept her for a few days. The social worker was concerned because Ms. Phillips never asked Mr. Farmer where he lived or when he was bringing Alexia back to the shelter. When Ms. Phillips was confronted, she told the social worker that he was Alexia's father and he would take care of her. She said,

"Even if he does not bring her back, she will be with her father." She reported that Mr. Farmer assists her financially on occasion by providing money and clothes for Alexia.

Recently, Ms. Phillips reported that she has a new boyfriend, whom she met since she has been living in the Third Chance Shelter. The social worker does not have his name, but was informed by Ms. Phillips that he is over the age of 40. Ms. Phillips reports that she is unable to have more children.

Keisha Phillips

Ms. Phillips is 22 years old. She has never been married. Her last name at birth was Stephens. Her mother, Daisy, married Kirk Phillips, and Kirk adopted Keisha. She was born in Chicago, Illinois, and lived there most of her life. She said that she moved to Jackson, Mississippi, shortly after the birth of KeKe and lived there with her aunt, Erline Phillips. She has two younger brothers who also reside with Erline and her husband, Levy Phillips.

Ms. Phillips parents, Kirk and Daisy Phillips, reside in Jackson, Mississippi. She stated that they live in a "crack house." According to Ms. Phillips, both her parents sell and use drugs (cocaine, heroin, methamphetamine). She states that she cannot live with them because they do not have water, electricity, or a phone. She indicates that her mother is under her father's thumb and reports that her mother does not know how to read or write and her father typically controls everything her mother does.

Ms. Phillips reported that her adopted father, Kirk, sexually abused her from age 7 up until she was 14 years old. She says that she forgives him and still talks to him, but would never leave her children alone around him. Her adopted father, Kirk, has two brothers, Levy (who is married to Erline) and Calvin. Calvin lives with Erline and Levy. According to Ms. Phillips, Calvin is a registered sex offender and was arrested for anal penetration of her daughter, KeKe, when KeKe was 3 years old. Ms. Phillips does not think that Levy Phillips, unlike his two brothers, would ever sexually abuse her children. She states that he is very loving to the children and would love for her and the children to move back and live with them.

Ms. Phillips reports that she did not graduate from high school. She says that she dropped out in tenth grade and started working at a fast food restaurant, but could not save any money because her parents were taking all of her money to support their drug habits. She stated that she was never encouraged to finish school and had to sneak to school because her parents wanted her to drop out and work to support the family. She states that she has had a hard time keeping a job because people on the job have always tried to take advantage of her, so she quits. She hopes to go to college one day to become a certified nurse's assistant. She would like to go to college so she can buy a house for her children.

KeKe

KeKe is 7 years old and in the second grade. According to Ms. Phillips, KeKe's teacher reports that KeKe has difficulty concentrating on school-work and spends most of her time daydreaming. The teacher also reports that KeKe makes Ds on most of her work, but she believes that KeKe is very smart. According to the teacher, KeKe appears to be a very needy child and loves attention and seeks praise. She states that KeKe is consistently late for school, often arriving after 10:00 a.m. Ms. Phillips says that this is her fault, because she has difficulty waking up in the morning. She says that if it were up to KeKe, she would be at school before the school opens. KeKe says she loves school.

Ms. Phillips says that KeKe is very disobedient to her and does not respect her. She says she always has to argue with KeKe over everything. Ms. Phillips says that KeKe cries all of the time and it gets on her nerves. She says that KeKe cries for no reason. KeKe has also had a lot of medical problems. She has been sexually abused all of her life and has sustained many injuries from the sexual abuse. She has also had a hernia behind her belly button since birth and will need to have surgery to have it repaired.

Jeremy

Jeremy is 4 years old and quite energetic. Jeremy does not listen to Ms. Phillips at all and typically misbehaves whenever he is with her. Jeremy has been observed engaging in inappropriate sexual behavior while at the shelter. Jeremy will often slap females on the buttocks or grab their breasts. The social worker states that on one occasion Jeremy crawled under the table and put his face between her legs. Ms. Phillips states that Jeremy has sex with KeKe's doll and she has told him to not do that. She states that she is not sure why he does it and she has punished him for it. The social worker has asked Ms. Phillips if it is possible that Jeremy has been sexually abused, and Ms. Phillips has stated that she does not think he has. The social worker has concerns that Jeremy may have been sexually abused as well. Keisha stated that Jeremy was questioned by the police and a social worker when KeKe was sexually abused, but he did not give any indication that he had been abused. After questioning the sleeping arrangements of the children, the social worker learned that Jeremy and KeKe sleep together.

Jeremy's fine motor and gross motor skills all appear to be within normal child development guidelines. Jeremy's communication/speech is a concern. He has a limited vocabulary for his age, and what speech he does demonstrate is typically slurred.

Alexia

Alexia is 15 months old and appears to be within the normal developmental guidelines for her age. Alexia walks fairly well. Alexia prefers her mother's sole attention, and is quick to draw away from or slap someone who approaches her. Alexia does not hesitate to get her mother's attention by crying if the older two siblings are treating her unfairly.

THE KIMBALL FAMILY

Student Instructions

You have been assigned to work with the Kimball family. You are a foster care case worker. Your caseload consists of cases where the parent or care taker has not complied with the treatment plan. You have been asked to assess this case and develop grounds for termination of parental rights due to continued environmental and physical neglect of the children.

Family Composition

The Kimballs are an African American family. The family consists of the parents, Jessie, age 30, and Delois, age 28. They have four children, Michael, age 8, Katerris, age 5, Marie, age 3, and Edward, who is 7 months old. Mr. Kimball is incarcerated and has been for six months. The family is receiving public assistance for all of the children. They are renting a two-bedroom house.

Current Situation

The Department of Children and Family Services (DCFS) went to the Kimball residence and found the home filthy and unfit for human habitation. The house was infested with roaches and mice, there was trash all over the floor, and the children stated that they did not have any running water. It was observed that there was exposed wiring running between two televisions and this presented an electrical hazard. The parents were not home, and there were no other adults in the home. The children did not know where their mother was or when she would return. They stated that she had been gone from home for three days. They stated that their father was in jail. Edward appeared to have a fever and was laying on the sofa without moving. The oldest child, Michael, stated that Edward had been sick. He also stated that he had no medicine to give him.

Michael knew his grandmother's phone number, and the protective services worker called the grandmother. The grandmother said that she would try and locate her daughter. The grandmother told the protective services worker that she could not care for the children. The children were taken into protective custody, and all of them were taken to the hospital for a checkup. Edward was hospitalized with pneumonia and severe diaper rash in the groin and abdominal areas. The other children had only minor colds. They were treated, released, and placed in a foster home.

Two days later, when the mother came home, she found a note from DCFS. She called to inquire about her children and was told that they had been placed in foster care. She immediately went to see her case worker. According to the case worker, the mother appeared intoxicated and explained that she had left the kids in the care of her oldest child, Michael.

Mrs. Kimball was arrested and charged with neglect of her children. When she went to court, the charges were dropped because she admitted having a problem with alcohol. She also admits experimenting with drugs on occasion. The judge ordered her into a thirty-day treatment program. The court recommended that she enter an alcohol treatment program at the local public hospital. While she was at the hospital, Dr. Dandridge diagnosed Mrs. Kimball as having alcohol and drug dependency, and it was recommended that she enter an intensive outpatient program or a residential program. She agreed to go into an outpatient program, but after two days there she dropped out and thereafter made no attempt to contact the Department of Children and Family Services.

After the children were taken into custody and the mother was placed in treatment, the family lost the home they were renting. Mrs. Kimball completed the thirty-day court-ordered program, but she did not complete the outpatient program. The case worker was unable to locate her for several months. Three months later, she called demanding to see her children. A visit was arranged for her to see her children. She stated that she was renting a room and was going to try to get an apartment so that her children could come home.

Mrs. Kimball came to visit her children and on the same day she attended an administrative case review to make plans for reunification with her children. At that time, she agreed to a service plan calling for her to successfully complete recommended treatment for chemical dependency, obtain and maintain housing adequate to accommodate the children, successfully complete a program of parenting classes, and maintain weekly visits with the children.

One week later, Mrs. Kimball dropped out of the intensive outpatient alcohol treatment program, and she has failed to participate further in any alcohol treatment program. Also, since the administrative case review, she has made no progress toward obtaining appropriate housing, has made no effort to participate in parenting classes, and has made no effort to see her children.

Family Background

This family was known to the Department of Children and Family Services prior to this incident. On several occasions the local police have found the children wandering the streets and have taken them home. On several occasions the police have escorted Mrs. Kimball home after finding her intoxicated on the street. The home had been observed to be in deplorable conditions on several other occasions. The parents have had a problem with alcohol and drugs since Katerris was born. Mr. Kimball has been in and out of jail for the past four years for burglary and drug possession. At this time he has been incarcerated for six months, and he received an eight-year sentence. He is currently in the city jail waiting to be processed, but he will be transferred to the state penitentiary. Mrs. Kimball was also arrested a year ago for writing bad checks. She served three months; a friend of hers came to the house and watched the children until she was released. Michael, the oldest son, also has a juvenile record. He was caught stealing some bread and lunch meat when he was 7 years old.

Mrs. Kimball has sporadically attended scheduled visits with the children. At each visit she made a lot of promises to the children, but she has never kept any of them. Although she calls to plan visits with the children on a monthly basis, in the last six months she has attended only three of them. On two of the visits Mrs. Kimball appeared intoxicated, and Michael was observed allowing Mrs. Kimball to lay her head in his lap while he comforted her.

Mrs. Kimball agreed to attend another case review to discuss plans for her children. Because she did not show up, the case worker visited the boarding home where she was living. Mrs. Kimball appeared to be sober. She was advised by the case worker that her continued failure to cooperate with service plan tasks could result in the filing of a petition to terminate her parental rights. However, Mrs. Kimball gave the case worker no indication that she would begin working toward the return of the children. A month later the case worker again met with Mrs. Kimball, at which time she had no plans regarding the children and stated no intent to pursue treatment for her continuing substance abuse. Since the children's entry into DCFS custody, the case worker has made several attempts to locate the maternal grandmother, but her whereabouts are unknown.

Michael

Michael, age 8, is healthy and developmentally on track. He is making good adjustment and appropriate progress in school and in his foster home. Michael worries a lot about his mother, and he has asked the foster mother if his mother could come and live with them. Michael is also worried about Edward and Marie, because they are in different foster homes. Michael misses Edward, because he has parented Edward since birth.

Katerris

Katerris is 5 years old. He is moderately mentally challenged, and his language development is severely delayed, to the extent that he is not verbal. Katerris is now starting kindergarten, and the extent to which he will be able to close his developmental gaps is not yet known. Michael and Katerris's current foster parents have no intention of adopting them even if they become available for adoption. The children miss their other siblings and hope they can be in the same home with them.

Marie and Edward

Marie and Edward have been placed in the same foster home. Marie is 3, generally healthy, and is making appropriate developmental progress. She catches colds very quickly; sometimes she has a difficult time breathing. Marie was a cocaine-addicted baby. The foster parents have very little knowledge about cocaine-addicted babies. Edward is 7 months old and was released from the hospital a month after birth. He had respiratory problems at birth and has had subsequent bouts with pneumonia, and he continues to experience asthma and respiratory difficulties. He was born with alcohol in his system. However, he is making good progress in placement, and his overall health is improving. He is a very friendly and happy baby. Marie and Edward's foster parents wish to adopt them in the event that they are ever available for adoption.

THE JONES FAMILY

Students Instructions

You are a school social worker assigned to work with child welfare cases The Jones family case has just come to your attention because a child (Kathy Jones) has missed three weeks of school and the mother failed to notify the school to report the child's absence. The school called Kathy's house every day, but no one answered the telephone. The truancy officer made four home visits, but no one answered the door, so the police forcefully entered the home. They found Kathy watching television, while the mother and two of her male friends were asleep.

Family Composition

The Jones's are a Caucasian family. The family consists of the mother, Pearl, age 35, her boyfriend, Marcus Pope, age 36, and Pearl's three children. Her daughter, Kathy, age 6, lives with her; her two other children, Gennie, age 9, and Paul, age 10, live with her maternal aunt, Ida Mae Simms, age 52. They live about twenty minutes away from Ms. Jones.

Current Situation

This pending case concerns Kathy. An investigation is currently under way of allegations that she may have been neglected by her mother. Kathy has not been to school in three-and-a-half weeks, and the mother did not notify the school of the child's absence. The school notified the Department of Children and Family Services (DCFS) because of Kathy's truancy. The mother, Pearl, has a history of substance abuse, but she has never been treated for it. Pearl has no open case with DCFS, but her other two children were placed in the guardianship of her aunt, Ida Mae Simms, after two cases of inadequate supervision were substantiated. Because Pearl did not follow through with a service plan with the department to return custody, DCFS requested that guardianship be given to the aunt and the DCFS case was closed. The aunt is retired and a widow. Her husband left her financially stable. Pearl receives public housing assistance and food stamps, and she works part time as a clerk in a local grocery store. The school reported that Kathy is always neat and clean when she is at school. Although she is absent a lot, she had never before missed three weeks of school. Recently, Mrs. Simms suffered a heart attack, and she states that she will not be able to care for Pearl's two other children. Pearl says that she wants to change her lifestyle so that she can obtain custody of her children, but she is very afraid to change.

Family Background

The Jones family resides in a public housing unit in a poverty-stricken community. The household consists of the mother, Pearl Jones, age 35, and her daughter, Kathy Jones, age 6. Marcus Pope, the children's father, who was recently incarcerated, will not be released for twenty years. A maternal aunt, Ida Mae Simms, lives twenty minutes away. Gennie and Paul Jones live with Mrs. Simms.

Pearl Jones

Ms. Jones has no siblings, and her mother died ten years ago of a drug overdose. She has not seen her father since her mother died. Pearl states that her mother is the reason that she uses drugs, because her mother was never there for her. She states that she practically raised herself because her mother was never at home. She likes her job but would like a full-time position. She is feeling disappointed because her boyfriend was recently sentenced to twenty years in prison, her aunt had a massive heart attack two weeks ago, and she was reported to DCFS for child neglect. She has two close friends, but they are substance abusers as well. She is not sure that she will be able to care for three children if she gets custody of them. She states that she wants to change her lifestyle because she wants to maintain custody of her children, but she is very afraid. She states that her aunt is the only family or support system that she has. Recently she has been sad most of the time.

Marcus Pope

Marcus Pope is 36 years old and was recently incarcerated for twenty years because of possession of narcotics with intent to sell. This was Marcus's third offense, so he was given the maximum penalty. Marcus spent more time with Kathy than with the other children. Mrs. Simms did not allow him at her home because Paul and Gennie do not want to be around him, but Kathy adores him.

Kathy

Kathy Jones is 6 years old and very quiet. She loves her mother, but she wants to see her brother and sister more often. She likes school and is a good student. After she finishes her work, she helps other students with theirs. She does not understand why she is often absent from school. She feels angry and upset at her mother when she does not go to school.

Ida Mae Simms

Ida Mae Simms is Pearl's maternal aunt. Recently, she suffered a massive heart attack. Now she just wants to relax, and she does not want the responsibility of Pearl's children. She stated that they are good children and that she loves them very much. However, she feels frustrated and thinks that Pearl should be responsible for all her children. She says that she has helped Pearl long enough and it is time for her to assume her role as a mother to her children. She states that Pearl should not continue to use drugs to deal with her problems.

Paul

Paul Jones is 10 years old and is very mature for his age. He helps his great aunt with chores and enjoys school. Paul's teacher says that he is an asset to her class. He feels sad because his great aunt is sick, but he feels that she will get better. He understands that he might have to live with his mother or possibly live in foster care. He does not want to leave his friends or his school. Paul states that he loves his mother, but he does not want to live with her or in foster care. Paul is very upset because he thinks that his aunt got sick because she had to take care of them, and he knows that his sister gives his aunt a lot of problems.

Gennie

Gennie Jones is 9 years old and is very nonchalant. She has two friends that her aunt dislikes because she feels that they are a bad influence. She wants to live with her mother because she feels that there will be fewer boundaries. She feels that her aunt is too old fashioned and smothers her. Gennie is barely an average student in school, and her aunt has to watch her practically all the time, so she can complete her homework. Gennie's teacher states that she is very disruptive in school and she must often call on her aunt to intervene. Gennie has been suspended several times this year for disrupting the class.

SAFETY AND RISK ASSESSMENT QUESTIONS

1. What forms of neglect are present in this family?

2. How do these forms of neglect impact the protection of the child or children in the family?

3. How does the issue of neglect determine intervention?

4. Does the neglect impact family preservation? Explain.

5. What cultural factors must be considered in the determination of what constitutes neglect in this family?

6. How do these factors impact your perception or ability to work with this family?

7. What resources are available or accessible to the family to reduce or prevent further neglect?

8. What community factors contribute to the presenting neglect issue?

FAMILY CASE ANALYSIS—ENGAGEMENT

1. What is the presenting problem? How are the family members involved in the situation defining the problem?

2. In exploring the situation, how does the information that you learn from other family members inform your perceptions?

3. How would you define the working problem based on the current information?

4. What strategies do you think would be useful in engaging with the individuals involved?

FAMILY ASSESSMENT

1. How would your definition of the working problem direct your assessment?

2. What assumptions about human and social behavior are you making, and how would you follow up with these?

3. Are there other problems or issues you think might emerge as you delve deeper into this case? What are they, and how might they affect the situation?

4. What information are you lacking about the situation and its context that you feel you need to know to gain an in-depth understanding?

5. Identify the strengths, limitations, and barriers present in this family. Based on the strengths, where would you start to work with this family?

6. What issues of motivation and/or resistance do you think you are likely to encounter? How do you think you might handle them?

7. Give a clear and concise summary of your assessment, and state how it affects the defining of general goals.

8. Identify and briefly state at least two theoretical frameworks or approaches that would guide your intervention in working with this family.

9. Prepare a genogram and an ecomap for the family, using the blanks given as Figures 3.1 and 3.2.

PLANNING FOR THE FAMILY

1. State your general goals in working with this family.

2. State specific objectives related to each goal, and identify specific changes in the situation that might lead to accomplishing the above goals.

3. What actions should be taken by the worker, the clients, or others to operationalize your objectives?

4. How are you going to set up your evaluation to track accomplishments or progress in goals and objectives? (*Note:* This section should reflect knowledge of methods of practice evaluation.)

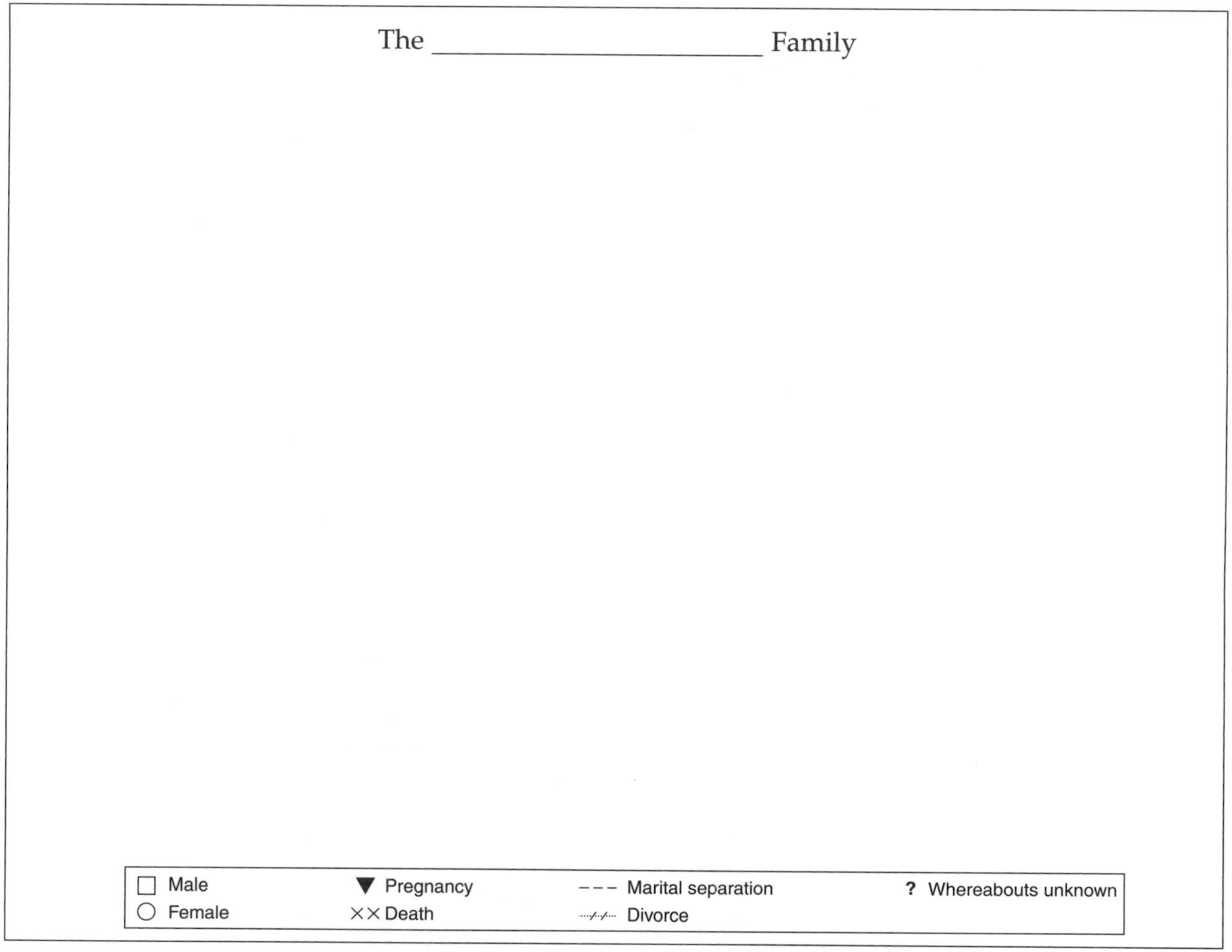

The _____ Family

Male
Female

▼ Pregnancy
× × Death

– – – Marital separation
––/–/–– Divorce

? Whereabouts unknown

FIGURE 3.1 The Family Genogram
(Sketch a genogram of the facts of this family structure.)

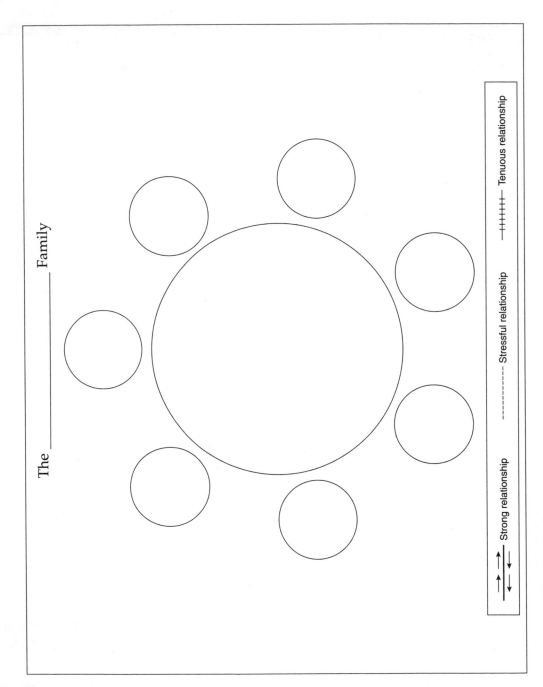

The _____ Family

Strong relationship

Stressful relationship

Tenuous relationship

FIGURE 3.2   The Family Ecomap

FAMILY TREATMENT PLAN/CONTRACT

Design a treatment plan for this family. This is an example of a treatment/contract plan. Most practice texts provide examples.

The Brown Family Treatment/Contract Plan

Client: _____ (Define the client here.)

I. **Brief Description of the Problem**
(This is generally a summary of the reasons the client came to you or your agency.)

II. **Primary Goals and Objectives** (Find a format that is clear to your client and you.)

    1. Goal:

         Objective:

    2. Goal:

         Objective:

    3. Goal:

         Objective:

III. **We, the undersigned, agree to the following tasks:**

    1.

    2.

IV. **Evaluation of Progress** (How your plan will be evaluated.)

_____   _____

_____   Signature of Social Worker

_____

Signature(s) of Client(s)

_____   _____

(Date)   (Date)

SUGGESTED READINGS

Azzi-Lessing, L., & Olsen, L. J. (1996). Substance abuse-affected families in the child welfare system: New challenges, new alliances. *Social Work, 41*(1), 15–23.

Brown, A. W., & Bailey-Etta, B. (1997). An out-of-home care system in crisis: Implications for African American children in the child welfare system. *Child Welfare 76*(1), 65–83.

Burnette, D. (1997). Grandmother caregivers in inner-city Latino families. *Journal of Multicultural Social Work, 5*(3/4), 121–137.

Coohey, C. (1998). Home alone and other inadequately supervised children. *Child Welfare, 77*(3), 291–310.

Cook, R. (1994). Are we helping foster youth prepare for their future? *Children and Youth Services Review, 16,* 213–229.

Cook-Loveland, C. A., Selig, K. L., Wedge, B. J., & Gohn-Baube, E. A. (1999). Access barriers and the use of prenatal care by low-income, inner city women. *Social Work, 44*(2), 129–139.

Gardner, R. A. (1997). An instrument for objectively comparing parental disciplinary capacity in child-custody disputes. *Journal of Divorce & Remarriage, 27*(3/4), 1–15.

Gaudin, J., & Sutphen, R. (1993). Foster care vs. extended family care for children of incarcerated mothers. *Journal of Offender Rehabilitation, 19*(3/4), 129–147.

Gebel, T. J. (1996). Kinship care and non-relative family foster care: A comparison of caregiver attributes and attitudes. *Child Welfare, 75* (1), 5–18.

Goldsmith, H. H., Buss, K. A., & Lemery, K. S. (1997). Toddler and childhood temperament: Expanded content, stronger genetic evidence for the importance of environment. *Developmental Psychology, 33*(6), 891–905.

Hairston, C. F., & Lockett, P. (1985). Parents in prison: A child abuse and neglect prevention strategy. *Child Abuse and Neglect, 9* 471–477.

Hicks, M. A. (1995). Shattered dreams: Ministering to parents after the loss of a child. *Journal of Family Ministry, 9*(1), 26–36.

Howell, S., Portes, P., & Barron, J. (1997). Gender and age difference in child adjustment to parental separation. *Journal of Divorce and Remarriage, 27*(3/4), 141–158.

Hunt, M. A. (1997). Comparison of origin factors between children of alcoholics and children of non-alcoholics in a longitudinal panel. *American Journal of Drug and Alcohol Abuse, 23*(4), 597–613.

Iglehart, A. P. (1995). Readiness for independence: Comparison of foster care, kinship care, and non foster care adolescents. *Children and Youth Services Review, 17*(3), 417–432.

Lewis, M., Giovannoni, J. M., & Leake, B. (1997). Two-year placement outcomes of children removed at birth from drug-using and non-drug-using mothers in Los Angeles. *Social Work Research, 21*(2), 81–90.

Petro, B. (1990). Boarder babies: Permanency planning and discharge status; a one year follow-up study of 100 infants placed in foster care. Fordham University, DSW Dissertation.

Rose, S. J., & Meezan, W. (1996). Child neglect: A study of the perceptions of mothers and child welfare workers. *Children & Youth Services Review, 17*(4), 471–486.

Rose, S. J., & Meezan, W. (1996). Variations in perceptions of child neglect. *Child Welfare, 75*(2), 139–160.

Scarf, M. (1997). *Intimate Worlds How Families Thrive and Why They Fail.* New York: Ballantine Books.

Warsh, R., & Pine, B. A. (1995). The meaning of family preservation: Shared mission, diverse methods. *Families in Society, 76*(10), 625–630.

Wells, K., & Tracy, E. (1996). Reorienting intensive family preservation services in relation to public child welfare practice. *Child Welfare, 75*(6), 667–692

■ ■ ■ ■ ■

CHAPTER FOUR

EMOTIONAL AND VERBAL ABUSE

THE DELANEY FAMILY

Student Instructions

You are an ongoing child protective services case worker in a child welfare agency. You have just received a case that was substantiated for emotional abuse, and the child protective services intake interviewer suspects that there may be other issues of child safety. Therefore, you have been directed to keep the case open for ninety days for further investigation and to monitor the initial case plan. The parents signed a case plan stating that they would go to counseling and parenting skills classes. The parents are somewhat resistant. They have admitted that they do have some problems, but they are cautious about what they share with you. Although they have consented to home visits, they are not very cooperative or forthcoming in giving information. They are aware that the investigator has strong feelings and reservations about their case. You have been given some information about the family, including the extended family, to help you analyze the case and work with the family to ensure child safety.

Family Composition

The Delaney family consists of the parents, Thomas, age 28, and Janice, age 27. They have twin daughters, Angelina and Abigail, who are 2 years old.

Current Situation

Mr. and Mrs. Delaney, a Caucasian couple, have been together for five years but have only been married for fourteen months. They have twin girls. The neighbors called the Department of Children and Family Services (DCFS) and reported that they have heard the parents use very harsh language toward the children. The neighbors report that they hear the children crying and that their cries do not sound normal. The neighbors also report that they have not seen the children in a week or so, and they are afraid the children are being harmed. A child protective services intake investigator investigated the case and substantiated the report of inappropriate parenting skills because, as punishment, the parents would lock the kids up in their room for hours. The parents rationale was that they did not want to hit the children. The father also stated that he would go two or three days and not talk to the girls, as a way of punishment. He also stated that he would not let the mother hold the girls or give them any kind of attention for a few days until they behaved better. The investigator felt that this family needed parenting skills and that there appeared to be other problems that would warrant a worker in the family to ensure child safety. The investigator did not feel comfortable closing the case and stated that the girls appeared in good health but small for their age. The girls' affect was of sadness, and they appeared to have distant looks on their faces. The investigator also felt that the parents seemed "too perfect" because they appeared to have calculated answers to all of his questions.

Family Background

The Delaneys live in a working-class neighborhood. Their annual income is about $35,000 a year. Mr. Delaney's parents were blue-collar workers and wanted much more for their children. On the other hand, Mrs. Delaney stated that she grew up in a family that was dependent on public assistance and really did not work much, but she was determined to have a better life. According to Mr. Delaney, his family has a very strong work ethic, but they believe that once you have a family, you are on your own.

Thomas Delaney

Mr. Delaney is employed as a sanitation worker. Lately, he has been having problems on the job. He says his boss does not know how to communicate with him, and he feels that his boss does not care about his employees. Mr. Delaney finds his worth and dignity in providing for his family. He is willing to fight at work for what he sees as an injustice. Recently, the company decided to cut some positions and lay off some people. Mr. Delaney heard that he might be one of the people who would be be laid off for six months. He states that, because of their financial situation, he cannot afford to be laid off or lose his job. He says he has attempted to talk to his boss, but his boss refuses to listen to him. He is very angry and has gone over his boss' head to the owner of the company. The owner told him that the company must downsize and he does not know who will be laid off or who will lose their jobs. Mr. Delaney states that he does not think he can handle the stress. Lately, he is beginning to spend a lot of time with co-workers after work, because he feels that he needs to unwind before he goes home. He finds himself drinking more than he would like to, but he does not consider his drinking excessive. Staying out late is beginning to cause problems in his marriage. However, he feels that until things get better at work, this is the only way he knows how to release some of his stress and deal with the situation. If he does come home right after work, he ends up getting upset and arguing with his wife.

His parents live nearby but do not provide much support to him or his family. He feels they see him as the son who does not need them, because he works hard and has always taken care of himself and his family. Although his family has always thought he made a mistake in becoming involved with Mrs. Delaney, they respect him for trying to make his marriage work. Mr. Delaney ignores the comments that his family makes about his wife and her family, and he cannot understand why they will not try and build a relationship with her.

Janice Delaney

Mrs. Delaney is a resilient woman who has faced many challenges in her life and completed college when no one thought she would. She works at the day care center that the twins attend. She states that she is forced to work at the center in order to pay for day care. She has a B.S. in business administration, but cannot seem to find a job in her field. She has often thought things might be better if they relocated, but Mr. Delaney refuses to leave the area where he grew up. Mrs. Delaney has recently learned that she might be pregnant, but she is afraid to tell her husband since he told her that they cannot afford another baby. She does not know what to do and cannot bear to tell him, considering everything that is happening on his job. She has been considering having an abortion without letting him know, but she is afraid to deceive him. She feels that an abortion might be her only alternative unless their financial situation improves. Mrs. Delaney's family lives down the street from her, but they provide no support to her at all. She also states that she must constantly explain to them that she cannot help them financially, because of her current financial situation. Her family views her as refusing to help them and tells her that she thinks she is better than they are. Mr. Delaney does not have a good relationship with her family and does not want them involved in their immediate family business.

Both parents state that they love and care about the girls. Both appear to care for and love each other and are struggling to keep their marriage and family together. They also state that they have a very strong work ethic.

Angelina

Angelina is the older of the twins. She was born ten minutes before Abigail. Angelina appears to be physically developed for her age, but she seems to be listless at times, and her affect is one of sadness. She seems shy around people and often hides under a chair. She does not speak to or look at strangers. According to the day care teacher, Angelina is very bright but shy, and she often becomes fearful when her father picks her up from the center. On several occasions Mr. Delaney has come to the day care.

Abigail

Abigail is the younger twin, smaller in size but more outgoing. According to the day care teacher, she seems different when Mr. Delaney picks her up. It has been brought to the parents' attention that the girls seem different when their father picks them up. According to the center, the parents' response to this was that the girls were playing a game. According to the parents, the game also included Abigail hitting her head against the wall over and over.

THE BENTON FAMILY

Student Instructions

You are a follow-up worker with the local child welfare agency, and you have been assigned to work with the Benton family. The intake investigator is transferring the case to your unit, because she could not substantiate the initial report of abuse. However, the investigator felt that some emotional abuse might be occurring. Adam, age 15, was sent to talk to the school counselor because he appeared depressed and had begun to isolate himself from the other students. The counselor contacted the school social worker, but Adam revealed nothing. However, based on the report from Adam's counselor, which stated that Adam appeared extremely depressed and had stopped eating, she filed a report with the Department of Children and Family Services (DCFS). Since your involvement, you have been able to get a little more information and now it is your responsibility to work with this family. The case will remain open for ninety days while you do a case analysis.

Family Composition

The Benton family consists of a single mother, Joyce, age 40, and her four children. There are two sons, Adam, age 15, and Tommy, age 10. The two daughters are Angel, age 13, and Tammy, age 12. Their father, Jeffery Benton, age 42, is involved in the family but is not in the home.

Presenting Problem

Mrs. Benton arrived home from work after midnight and found the house in disarray. She was so angry that she woke Tommy and Angel and asked them what happened. They explained that Adam had told them not to worry about cleaning the house or helping with supper. He just wanted them to go to bed. She sent them back to bed and cleaned the house herself. The next morning, Adam noticed that his mother was upset with him. He tried to explain to her what had happened, but she told him that she did not want to hear anything he had to say and wanted him out of her sight. She said, "Adam, you will grow up to be as trifling and irresponsible as your father. I cannot believe I trust you to do anything right. I will never trust you to care for the children or expect anything other than ignorance from you. Angel will be the person in charge from this day forward when I go to work, because she is responsible and is much more intelligent than you." After Adam's conversation with his mother he became even more depressed and is now seriously contemplating taking his own life.

Current Situation

Joyce Benton is currently raising her four children by herself. Mrs. Benton has just taken on a second job and is not at home in the evenings. The children are being asked by their mother to assume roles and responsibilities they have not taken on in the past. Since Adam is the oldest, he is in charge when she is not home. Adam is not handling this responsibility as well as his mother expects him too. His siblings do not respect him as an authority figure when their mother is not home. Mrs. Benton is very frustrated and has started using extreme profanity toward the children. Adam has told his best friend that maybe things would be better if he killed himself.

Family Background

The Bentons are a Caucasian working-class family. Mr. and Mrs. Benton were married for fifteen years. The Bentons have been separated for five years. However, Mr. Benton has maintained a relationship with the children and has supported them financially. Six months ago, Mr. Benton moved to another city, and he did not leave a forwarding address. Mrs. Benton is feeling the stress of suddenly being a single parent and having to work two jobs to support her children. When the Bentons were married, their family income was about $70,000 a year. After Mr. Benton moved out, he still paid child support, which was a help to Mrs. Benton and the children. Now, they are depending entirely on Mrs. Benton's income, which is only about $30,000 per year.

The Bentons met in college and married about a year after they met. They felt they were in love, and both wanted children. They thought they had a fairly good relationship but they have had many problems; however, they agreed not to share their problems with the children. Mrs. Benton has never told Jeffery about the baby she gave up for adoption. She says that she never wanted to break his heart. Mrs. Benton is not really close to her own family, and during their marriage she did not bond with Mr. Benton's family. As a matter of fact, she thinks that Mr. Benton's family is too close. On the other hand, Mr. Benton was very close to Mrs. Benton's parents. He had a special relationship with her mother and often tried to bring Mrs. Benton and her mother together. Mrs. Benton does wish, however, that she had allowed her children to bond with her parents before her mother died two years ago.

Joyce Benton

Joyce is a 40-year-old woman who has had her share of problems in life. She had her first child when she was 15 years old. Her parents made her put the child up for adoption. She never wanted to put her child up for adoption, but felt she was pressured by her parents. In a lot of ways, she has not forgiven them. She says her parents saw her as a disappointment after she got pregnant, and they did not support her after her sophomore year in high school. In fact, she remembers her mother calling her names and constantly telling her, "Joyce, you will never be anything. Joyce, look at you! You are one big disappointment." She says that after that ordeal she decided that she would prove to her mother that she could become somebody. She finished college with honors even though her parents did not even come to her college graduation. She has an older brother and sister whom her parents see as very successful. She does not communicate with her family often and has not seen any of them for about five years.

Mrs. Benton admits that she might not be the best parent, but she has never walked out on her children. She loves her children but does not think they love her. She feels that the children have always favored their father, and she knows that they blame her that he left home. She is very angry at her husband for walking out on them. She says that she was determined to earn a college degree, even though her parents did not support her either emotionally or financially. Therefore, she feels she will make it without her husband. Joyce sees herself as a survivor and feels that life has not been fair to her.

Mrs. Benton's best friend, Jason, lives in another part of the country. She says they met in college and for some reason he always understood her. She says it was Jason who encouraged her to marry Jeffery. Jason is married, and his wife is very jealous of their relationship, so she rarely calls him but knows he is thinking of her and would help her out if she called on him.

Jeffery Benton

Jeffery is a 42-year-old man who grew up in a very close-knit family. Jeffery has three older sisters, one younger brother, and one younger sister. His parents were very supportive of him all of his life. He met Joyce in college and says that he fell in love with her. He says she had dreams and was a "go-getter" even though she had no support from her parents. He says, "Joyce has a lot of anger and expects people in her life to disappoint her." He feels that during their marriage he tried very hard to please her, but it was very difficult. There were times when Joyce would go days without talking and he would not know why. He would try and talk to her and she would only say, "Jeffery, you have had a perfect life, you could not begin to understand my life."

Mr. Benton says that after their first two children were born, Joyce became verbally abusive to him and would be very emotional. He asked her to go to counseling and she refused, thinking he was accusing her of being crazy. After Tammy was born things got a little better, but when Tommy came along, she completely isolated Tommy and her husband. He recalls the day he left the house for good. He says that it was a beautiful day and it was Tommy's birthday. They had planned a big birthday party for him. She came home from work and locked herself in the bedroom and refused to interact with anyone. He says that the children were sad but he encouraged them to continue with the party. After the party he attempted to talk to her, but she said the only thing that would make her happy was for him to leave the house. He told her that if he left he would not return. He says that it broke his heart to leave his home and his children. But he made a decision and left. He wanted to take the kids but she refused. He continued to support the kids financially but felt that he did not have anything to give them emotionally. He says he was emotionally drained by the time he moved out.

Four years ago, he met someone and has fallen in love. He has asked Mrs. Benton for a divorce but she refuses. He does not blame his wife for all of their problems. He does admit having had an affair about four years after Tommy was born, but states that he and Joyce had not been involved intimately since Tommy was a year old. He wishes he could tell her and the children where he has moved, but he is afraid that she would destroy his new life. He has talked to his family, and his mother and siblings have told him they would help him if he took custody of the children. However, he feels that if he takes the children from Joyce, it would kill her: they are all she has. He also realizes that the children must be very unhappy because of their parents' breakup.

Adam

Adam is 15 years old and the oldest child. He looks very much like his father. When he was born, he was the apple of his mother's eye, but now he feels that he can do nothing to please her. She always seems disappointed in him. She takes everything out on him because she feels he should be taking care of the house while she is at work. Adam is unsure of exactly what his mother expects from him, but knows he is responsible for everything. He has become very nervous and is starting to have "blackouts." He wants to see a doctor but his mother does not have enough money to take him. Adam is a good student; he is not an A student, but does his best. Recently, one of his teachers noticed that he was having difficulty concentrating and his grades were dropping, so she sent him to talk to the school counselor.

Adam is confused as to why his father left without giving them his address. He does remember his father and mother having an argument about a week before his father moved, but does not know what the argument was about. Adam says his father is not aware of how they are feeling or how his mother is treating them. He feels that if his father was aware, he would come and get them. He has his grandmother's phone number and has wanted to call her, but he knows that his mother would be very angry if he did.

Angel

Angel is 13 years old and the second child. She rarely goes against what her mother tells her and is an excellent student. She gets good grades and also gets most of her mother's attention. Angel is not liked very much by her siblings because she tells her mother everything. She also calls her siblings derogatory names, and does everything she can to obtain approval from her mother. However, she has told her friends that if it was not for Adam, she would not have a chance to do after-school activities and that she loves Adam very much.

Tammy

Tammy is 12 years old and the third child. She is quiet and basically keeps to herself. No one seems to pay much attention to Tammy. She does her own thing. Recently Adam found her having sexual intercourse with a boy from the neighborhood. He is afraid to tell his mother, because she will be angry and blame him. Tammy says she hates her mother, because her mother calls her derogatory names. Tammy is a very good student at school and is liked by most of her teachers. Tammy was very close to her father, and she blames her mother for her father's leaving.

Tommy

Tommy is 10 years old and the youngest child. He is very playful and tries to keep everyone laughing and joking. He is a slow learner and has been diagnosed as hyperactive. He gets very little attention from his mother, because she says she cannot deal with him. He was somewhat close to his father, but he sees Adam almost like a father. He really depends on Adam, and whenever there is something going on at his school, Adam takes him. Adam has also walked him to school since he was in kindergarten. He is upset that Adam is not happy and he tries to cheer Adam up.

THE HAWKINS FAMILY

Student Instructions

You are working in a child welfare agency and have been assigned a case of a child who is refusing to go home from the hospital. Terrance Scott, age 12, was admitted to the hospital about ten days ago for attempted suicide. He is ready for release but is terrified of returning home. Although the hospital social worker has spoken with him, he did not disclose why he is afraid to return home. The hospital social worker called in the report, as he is concerned that there is more to the situation than Terrance has disclosed. The hospital social worker recommended that the family attend counseling, but the family did not appear interested, nor have they made a commitment to go.

Family Composition

The Hawkins family consists of the parents, Dennis, who is Caucasian and 56 years old, and Jessica, an African American who is 48 years old.

They have three children. Dewayne, age 15, is their adopted son. Terrance Scott, age 12, is Mrs. Hawkins's biological son, and Beverly, age 10, is Mr. Hawkins's biological daughter.

Current Situation

Their children are experiencing a lot of emotional problems. This is not Terrance's first attempt to commit suicide. He is currently in the hospital but is ready for discharge and is refusing to return home. The hospital is willing to keep Terrance a few more days until an assessment is made. The parents are very upset and do not understand why Terrance does not want to come home. Both parents state that they love Terrance. Mrs. Hawkins has been feeling depressed and frustrated. She feels that her life has been a big disappointment. Mr. Hawkins has been drinking excessively and has a lot of bad feelings toward his wife for cheating on him after eight "good" years of marriage. They have been to family court on disorderly conduct and domestic violence charges. They have also gone to marriage counseling, but did not disclose any information about the counseling to the therapist.

Present Family Relationships

The Hawkinses did not believe that they could have children, so they adopted Dewayne. Dewayne is the oldest child and was their first child. In their eyes, he has been a blessing to them, because according to Mr. Hawkins he binds them together. Three years after Dewayne was adopted, Mrs. Hawkins had an affair and became pregnant with Terrance. She did not tell Mr. Hawkins that he was not the father until after the baby was born and the child did not look anything like Mr. Hawkins. During her pregnancy Mr. Hawkins bonded with the baby, and he is very disappointed that Terrance is not his child. However, he has raised him as his own. Two years after Terrance was born, Mr. Hawkins had an affair and his daughter Beverly was born. Beverly does not live with the Hawkins family, but she visits very frequently and spends most of the summer with the Hawkinses. Mrs. Hawkins is still bitter about Mr. Hawkins cheating on her, but she has a fairly good relationship with Beverly. The parents both state that up until three years ago, their relationship with their children was good. They go on to say that they are not sure when everything went bad. Dewayne is threatening to run away, because he does not like to see his parents fight, drink, and verbally abuse each other.

Mrs. Hawkins does not get along with Mr. Hawkins's family. She states that his parents do not like her because she is African American. Mr. Hawkins states that he got along very well with Mrs. Hawkins's parents when they were alive and still maintains a good relationship with her sister. They both say that they love each other very much, but Mrs. Hawkins says that Mr. Hawkins's drinking is causing the problems in the family. Mr. Hawkins, on the other hand, says that her lying and cheating are causing the problems. Mr. Hawkins admits that he does drink a little too much, but that it is not that bad. He states that he has had only three DUIs and according to him, two of them were false. According to the hospital social worker, Mr. Hawkins has appeared intoxicated on two occasions when he visited Terrance.

Family Background

Mr. and Mrs. Hawkins have been married for twenty years. They are both currently unemployed. Mr. Hawkins says that he receives a monthly veteran's pension. Mrs. Hawkins states that she is currently on unemployment but will be receiving her last check in two weeks. They are currently receiving food stamps. She says that she is seeking employment, but feels she is too depressed to get out of bed and look for a job. They feel that they started having children too late in life and now they are in a trap. Both state that they have disappointed each other, but they do not seem to know why Terrance is having so many problems. They are experiencing real financial problems and cannot afford to continue to pay the doctor bills for Terrance. Terrance does not know anything about his biological father except his name. Mrs. Hawkins refuses to let him be involved in Terrance's life. She told Terrance that she gave him his biological father's name in case Mr. Hawkins ever got mad and didn't want to be his father anymore.

The entire family is socially withdrawn, and most of their extended family live out of town. Mrs. Hawkins states that she is in good health besides her depression. Mr. Hawkins has had three operations on his shoulder in the last two years. He feels that the doctors did not perform his operations correctly, and he is thinking about suing the hospital.

Mrs. Hawkins has one older sister and reports that they are very close. According to Mrs. Hawkins, she talks to her sister at least once a day. She reports that her sister used to live near her, but decided to take a job on the West Coast. She states that her parents are deceased and the only person who ever really cared about her was her sister. She also says that her mother was always sick and suffered with depression and so she was never very close to her. She reports that her father was a truck driver and stayed on the road all of the time, so she did not have the opportunity to build a relationship with him either.

Mr. Hawkins is the oldest of six siblings, four boys and two girls. He reports having had to be a parent to all of his siblings. He states that his mother died when he was 16. Before she died, she asked him to look after everyone and not to let the state separate them. He is especially close to his youngest two sisters, because they were infants when his mother died. His father was in and out of the house most of his life. He states that his father had a drinking problem and did not care for them. He also says that his father died about a year ago and did not leave anything to him. All of his father's possessions were left to his brother, Ben, who is an attorney. Ben has promised to give Dennis the money to make a new start, but only if he divorces Mrs. Hawkins. He is very angry with his brother Ben, because he put Ben through law school. He states that his other two brothers are angry that he married outside his race, and they will not even visit him. He has a very good relationship with his sisters, and they see him as their father. They have tried to build a relationship with the children, but it is difficult because when there are family functions Dennis's brothers will only allow Beverly to attend.

Initial Assessment of Family

Mr. and Mrs. Hawkins appear to want to stay together. Mrs. Hawkins feels much ambivalence about their relationship, due to her husband's alcohol problem. Mr. Hawkins reports that he had his first drink at the age of 21, which was thirty-five years ago. He reports that his drinking "habit" has increased from a half-pint of gin every two weeks to a pint of gin daily. He states, "maybe he will stop drinking," but does not feel he is an alcoholic, because his father was an alcoholic and drank a lot more than he ever could. He remembers that on one occasion he tried to stop drinking and he felt funny. He says he saw things and was shaking. He also says that if Mrs. Hawkins would stop "nagging" him about things he can't do anything about, it would help his drinking habit. Mrs. Hawkins's affect was of sadness and frustration. She appeared overwhelmed by household and financial responsibilities. For example, she said, "If it was not for me, we would not have a place to live or food to eat." She states that she is tired as she has been in this emotionally abusive relationship for twenty years. Both parents feel that they have learned from this experience that Terrance is refusing to come home, but that they were not aware that their lives and home were so uncomfortable for the boys.

Mrs. Hawkins thinks that Mr. Hawkins needs professional help for his "problem." Both state that they were embarrassed that after twenty years of marriage they might need family counseling. They are also upset that Terrance does not want to come home and that Dewayne is thinking of moving away from them. They report that they are somewhat angry at the boys, because they feel that they have always provided for them and now that they have problems the boys are ready to bail out on them. Mrs. Hawkins states that maybe they waited too long to bring children into their lives, because "it appears that the children today do not care about their parents."

Terrance

Terrance is very withdrawn and very clear that he cannot go back home now. He says that he has tried on several occasions to kill himself and the hospital always sends him back home. He says that the staff at the hospital has told him that he should want to go home, because he has such wonderful parents. He wishes he knew his real father but thinks that is impossible, since his mother will not give him any information. He says he does not know what to do, because he feels frustrated all the time.

Dewayne

Dewayne is very friendly, but his affect is one of frustration. He states that he loves his parents but does not know what to do with them. He says he is not so sure why they had children, since they constantly bring up that they do not know why they had children at such a late time in their lives. He feels responsible for everyone. He also states that when he leaves home he goes to one of his friends' houses, because their parents really like him and it is peaceful over there. He reports that on a couple of occasions, when his parents were fighting, he jumped in to help his mother and his father became so angry that he pulled a gun on Dewayne. He says that when that occurs, his father is genuinely sorry and each time promises never to do it again. He does not think his father will really hurt him, and he does not feel afraid of him. He says that he understands why Terrance does not want to come home and wishes that his parents would get their act together so that Terrance will feel more comfortable about returning home. He feels that he has a good relationship with both Terrance and Beverly.

Beverly

Beverly is 10 years old and appears to be very happy but finds it difficult to live in such a diverse family. She states that she is glad that she lives with her mother, but hates the fact that her mother does not like African Americans. She says her mother only allows her to visit her father because the courts make her. Also, she says that her father does pay child support. She feels that her mother really loves her father and has asked him to get a divorce and live with them. Beverly says she would love that, but she would hate to see her father leave her stepmother. She goes on to state that her mother told her that when her father was with her he stopped drinking and started going to church. Beverly states she loves both of her brothers but often feels caught in the middle, because she has a relationship with her dad's family and they do not. She says she asked her mother if Terrance could live with them, but her mother refuses and says she does not want to get involved with "those people." Beverly feels especially close to Terrance, because she lived with them for her first five years and she and Terrance grew up together.

THE WALLACE FAMILY

Student Instructions

You are working in a public child welfare office as an ongoing protective services worker. Your job is to try and keep families intact. Your office received a call from the police department stating that they had gone out on a domestic violence call and found two children living in what they consider a violent situation. They transported the mother, Selina Wallace, and her two children to the battered women's shelter and her boyfriend, Kenneth Thomas, was taken to jail. They would like the department to look into this situation and make an assessment. The department sent investigators out and they felt the children were safe now. However, it appeared to them that the mother was planning to return to the situation, although she told them that she was afraid to return home at this time. Ms. Wallace did not want to press charges against her boyfriend. However, the police decided to press charges because this was the fourth time they had been called to that residence for a domestic dispute. The police initially started to remove the children, but instead made a referral to your office and your office has decided to open the case as an ongoing protective services case and try to work with this family.

Family Composition

The Wallace family consists of the mother, Selina, age 28, and her two children, Gloria, age 7, and Camilla, age 4. Ms. Wallace's boyfriend, Kenneth Thomas, age 30, also lives in the home and is the father of Camilla. The maternal grandmother, Katherine Jackson, is involved in the family but does not live in the home. She lives about thirty minutes away from the family.

Current Situation

Ms. Wallace has been in this relationship with her boyfriend for six years. He has always been somewhat abusive. However, in the last two years he has become violent over many things. He has broken her leg and her arm. She is concerned because the last time he got angry, Gloria started to scream and begged him to stop and he slapped her. He begged her not to tell anyone and said he would never hit the children again. She says she loves him and does not want to leave him. He is the only father her children have known. Her mother is very frustrated with her because she continues to return to the situation. Her mother is also afraid of Kenneth. Selina knows that she should leave Kenneth but feels that she cannot just walk out on him. He is the financial provider for the family, and he contributes all of his money to the household. They attend church, and Kenneth is well liked and respected. Selina feels that at least she has a man who works and cares for his family. Most of her friends do not have a man, and they are on welfare or some type of public assistance. She considers herself lucky or blessed just to have someone in her life to help raise her children.

According to Selina, Kenneth told her that if he ever got locked up she had better "look out." Selina thinks he might kill her and the children, because he told her no one interferes with his family. He also told her that if he ever has to take money out of his children's mouth to pay for court because of her, he is not sure what he will do. Selina says she cannot walk out on him: he has no one else. Selina states that Kenneth's family is not supportive, and that he has always wanted a family and she cannot take this from him. She thinks his attorney is trying to get probation for him if he agrees to go to counseling. However, Kenneth told her that he would rather do his time than go and see a "shrink," because he is not "crazy." Selina thinks maybe if the case worker demands that he go to counseling, he will listen. She feels that the case worker must find a way to make him understand how serious this is and also how much his family needs him.

Family Background

The Wallace family resides in a lower-middle-class neighborhood, in a newly renovated townhouse. They are currently renting but hope to buy their own home someday. Selina had her own home that her father left her, but Kenneth made her sell it because he thought it would be best if they started from scratch together. She regrets selling the only thing her father left her but is afraid to tell Kenneth how she feels.

Kenneth Thomas

Mr. Thomas is the fourth of seven children. He has three older brothers and three younger sisters. He is employed as a construction worker, a seasonal job. When he is not working construction, he does odd jobs. He always wanted to attend college, but his family are primarily blue-collar workers and would not assist him financially. His father was in and out of the house during his childhood. He remembers that whenever his father was there, he constantly argued with his mother. He never really understood why his mother took so much abuse from his father, and he vowed that he would never be like his father. He is not close to any of his family. He visits his mother on occasion, but he refuses to talk to his father. He will not let Selina take the girls to see his family. He admits to hitting her but says she provokes him. He does not see himself as violent, and he despises men who beat women for no reason. He does not talk to people about his problems, and he has told Selina to keep people out of their family business.

Selina Wallace

Ms. Wallace is an only child and a stay-at-home mom. She would like to work, because she went to college and received a B.S. degree in Biology. "I have always wanted a family and a man to work with me." She is feeling very disappointed in her boyfriend, because he promised to marry her about three years ago but each year he puts it off. She feels that their relationship is not as good as it was, but she is afraid to bring it to his attention. She was once a very happy young lady, but lately she finds herself feeling sad most of the time. She has left her boyfriend before, but she never had to go to a shelter. She hopes that maybe this is not the end of their relationship and that maybe now they can go to counseling, but she does not know how to convince him. She knows that he is a good provider and loves them all. Selina thinks her mother would take the girls until she could work things out, but Kenneth told her that the girls cannot stay with her mother. She feels her choices are limited as to what she can do.

Gloria

Gloria is 7 years old and appears somewhat slow. School personnel have given her a number of tests but do not seem to be able to find any problems. She just does not perform in the classroom. Her teacher is concerned about her, because she stays alone and does not want to play with the other children. Sometimes, the teacher says, Gloria does not want to go home. The teacher has talked to her mother, but no one seems to know what the problem is. She loves Kenneth, calls him "Daddy," and always tries to please him. She wishes her parents would not fight. She enjoys baby dolls and has a lot of imaginary friends.

Camilla

Camilla is 4 years old and seems very happy. She laughs all the time and is very close to her mother. Camilla really enjoys playing with Barbie dolls and dressing up in adult clothes. She does not know what is going on in the family. She is having too much fun playing and creating imaginary friends.

Extended Family

Katherine Jackson is Selina's mother. She lives approximately half an hour away from her daughter. She has supported her daughter and does not know why her daughter got mixed up with someone like this guy. She says, "Selina never saw me mix with any low-life people. I told her he was not any good and she moved in with him anyway. I have taken her and the children in so many times and have begged her not to go back. I give up, and she is on her own. She will go back to him for sure. I want peace in my life. She should kill the 'son of a _____.'" She feels sorry for her grandchildren and says that she will take them in, but not her daughter. She is financially stable, because her husband left her plenty of money when he died. She states that her husband left Selina a nice savings account too, but Selina cannot access it until Gloria goes to high school. She says that she would help Selina out financially if she was assured that she would not go back into that abusive relationship.

THE HUMPHREY FAMILY

Student Instructions

You are a social worker with the Department of Children and Family Services (DCFS). You work in the foster care unit and have been with the agency for ten years. You have been working with two brothers, Edwin and Robert, since they came into foster care six years ago. Edwin has been diagnosed as mentally disabled, and his brother Robert is incarcerated for murder. Both boys remain in the custody of the state. You will need to find placement for Edwin because his foster parent, Mrs. Sterling, cannot keep him any longer. Edwin has been in Mrs. Sterling's home for six months since the death of her husband. She just does not think she can care for him alone. She also relied a lot on Robert to help with Edwin. Edwin is having nightmares and is grieving for his brother. Mrs. Sterling is grieving for her husband. She wants to make sure a good place is found for Edwin, but he will need to leave soon. Robert has confessed to murder but has not been sentenced.

Family Composition

The Humphrey family consists of Edwin, age 13, and his brother, Robert, age 16. The Humphrey boys reside in the foster home of Josephine Sterling, age 53. Josephine's husband, Max Sterling, age 57, was murdered six months ago by his foster son, Robert. Robert is currently incarcerated and awaiting sentencing.

Current Situation

Edwin and his brother Robert were emotionally, verbally, and physically neglected by their mother. Their mother left them in an apartment and told them "do not come out." She never returned for them. They were found by the maintenance man when he went to change the filter in the air conditioner. The boys told him that they had not seen their mother for a month. He called the police. The children were placed in foster care and have been there for six years. The mother was found a year later, and she stated that she did not want the boys and could not care for them. She promised to come in and talk to the foster care worker, but she never showed up. Their father was located; he was incarcerated under a life sentence for murder. Their parental rights were terminated two years ago. Edwin remains very close to his older brother Robert. Robert shot and killed his foster father. No one other than Robert knows the real reason for the shooting. Robert has acknowledged repeatedly that he shot his foster father, but he will not divulge the reason. The foster mother has been taking Edwin to visit Robert on a regular basis.

Family Background

Edwin is an African American male who has been in the care of the state for six years. He has been in the Sterling foster home since he came into care. Edwin has had three placement changes during his six-year history as a foster child. One placement change was from his initial emergency placement to a regular foster home, the other placement changes were for respite so that his foster parents could take vacation. The permanency goal for Edwin remains adoption, but he has had only one potential parent express interest in adopting him, and that person never submitted to a home study because he could not take two boys and the boys did not want to be separated. Because Edwin's permanency goal remains adoption, an adoption mentor has also been assigned to him. Although this person has not yet established a firm relationship with Edwin, it is hoped he will begin to put in the time necessary to do so.

Edwin was referred for counseling because of his behaviors, such as verbally threatening others, setting abandoned houses on fire, and one incident of killing a puppy. His therapist comes to the home weekly, and Edwin participates cooperatively with him. However, there remain unanswered questions regarding Edwin's behaviors, motivations, and underlying problems, which impede progress in therapy.

Edwin's birth mother had a serious history of alcoholism. The extent of drinking she engaged in while pregnant is unknown. When he was first placed in care Edwin reportedly masturbated excessively and would try to look under the dresses of women or girls. Mrs. Sterling thought that maybe Edwin had been sexually molested as a child. Edwin was evaluated and diagnosed as "mentally retarded." He was assessed as functioning at a 16-month-old level when he was 6 years old.

Edwin was placed in a class for the mentally disabled at an elementary school when he was 7. He is now in junior high school and is in advanced mentally disabled classes learning basic counting, how to spell his name, social skills, and cultural awareness. Edwin often has moments when he will start to cry and it is difficult for the teacher to get him to stop. Edwin is a very likable young man. He is warm, friendly, and loves attention.

Edwin is seen as a child who will be able to function in a sheltered workshop and supervised group home setting as an adult. Referrals to programs and situations in the next year or two that will provide exposure to and assistance in learning independent living skills will help prepare Edwin for a more independent adult life. Edwin is able to attach to others, and this ability to attach and to be part of a group is one of his greatest strengths. Currently his strongest attachments are to his brother and his foster mother. Edwin also speaks very positively regarding his classroom teacher and his current therapist. These are all adults, however (except for his 16-year-old brother), and currently Edwin does not seem to have any strong attachments to other children, although he has at times in the past had friends who were important to him.

Any assessment of Edwin would of course need to take into account the fact that he has limited intellectual ability and has few supports available to him when he is away from the foster parent's home or away from the classroom.

Robert

Robert is 16 years old and is currently incarcerated for the murder of his foster father. Robert was 10 when he first came into custody. According to his records, his mother used to leave him and his brother, Edwin, in drug houses; on two occasions his mother admitted to trading him for drugs when he was 2 years old. Robert has always been the caretaker for Edwin. Robert is concerned about what will happen to Edwin, because he was told by someone that he might get life in prison. Robert is also concerned because he feels he disappointed his foster mother. Robert has confessed to the murder. According to Edwin, Mr. Sterling hurt them. Neither Edwin nor Robert will go into any details or explain what they mean by "hurt." A public defender has been appointed for Robert, and he has been charged as an adult. His public defender has done some volunteer work for abused and neglected children, and he thinks something happened to Robert while in the Sterling home. He would like to obtain a different charge for Robert.

Josephine Sterling

Josephine is a 53-year-old woman who had been in an abusive marriage for twenty-five years. When she got married, her husband moved her 1,000 miles away from her family. Josephine has two older brothers and two younger sisters. According to Josephine, her husband Max was not abusive to her for the first two years of their marriage. She states that he was a lonely man and never wanted children. For years she wanted children or to adopt, but he prohibited her from having children. About seven years ago he agreed to go with her to foster parent classes. She always thought if she had some children he would stop beating her. When she took Edwin and Robert into her home, it changed her life. She says she has never been so happy. She wanted to adopt them when they became free for adoption, but her husband would not allow her to. She states that on occasion her husband would get angry because of all the attention she gave the boys. She remembers that on one occasion Edwin and Robert cried after her husband beat her and she had to go to the hospital. She sustained six broken ribs, one broken arm, and a cut lip and eye. She says that when she came home from the hospital Robert told her, "Mama, the next time he beats you like that I am going to kill him." She says she told Robert that he should never hurt anyone. She says that she asked her husband not to be violent or angry in front of the boys from that moment on. She still feels committed to the boys and blames herself for what Robert did. She says her husband was never very close to the boys and she tried to make sure that he did not hurt them.

She remembers on occasion taking a beating for the boys. She says the boys never called Max "Daddy" or "Father." She is very confused and feels somewhat angry at Robert but knows that he is a good child. She does not want to turn her back on him but is not sure she can be his "Mama" anymore. She and Edwin continue to visit Robert on a weekly basis. She states that she and Edwin do not talk about things and their house climate has changed. She says that she has observed Edwin regress since Robert has been incarcerated, and she cannot help him.

THE HERNANDEZ FAMILY

Student Instructions

You are a social worker for a private child welfare agency. The Hernandez family was referred to your agency by the Department of Children and Family Services (DCFS). The department investigated a case of emotional abuse but could not substantiate the allegations. They referred the family to your agency for an assessment. The investigator suspects that there may be some emotional neglect, domestic violence, and other unidentified family issues.

Family Composition

The Hernandez family consists of the parents, Antonio and Andrea, both 40 years old. They have three children, a son, Reuben, age 15, and two daughters, Sonia, age 10, and Rosa, age 5. The maternal and paternal grandparents are involved with this family. The maternal grandparents are Ricardo and Agustina Bennetti, and the paternal grandparents are Alcevedo and Patricia Hernandez.

Current Situation

Mrs. Andrea Hernandez called the Women's Crisis Center and asked for assistance. She stated that she was afraid of her husband. After he returned home intoxicated, her husband demanded that she cook. When she refused, he hit her in the face and threw her out of the house. The children were awakened and were afraid for their safety because Mr. Hernandez was throwing things around the house. The children cried and begged him to allow their mother to stay in the house. He then made all of the children get their mother's belongings and throw them outside on the porch. When their son refused, Mr. Hernandez grabbed him and pulled him, and threatened to put him out of the house with his mother. The children were crying and he screamed and told them to stop crying. He then made their daughter Sonia go in the kitchen and cook him a meal. After two hours he fell asleep. The children then let their mother back into the house. They were all nervous and upset over the ordeal. Mrs. Hernandez says this time was the worst and that he has never been this destructive before.

Family Background

The Hernandezes are a middle-class Latino family. Both parents work, and they provide the family with a comfortable living environment. They live in the suburbs in a single-family home. They are financially stable and are instilling in their children the importance of having a strong work ethic. Mrs. Hernandez has been the victim of domestic violence for about ten years. She has sustained a broken nose, broken arm, and many black eyes. She has tried to keep their fighting away from the children, but they are aware of the problems because Mr. Hernandez's violent episodes have progressed.

The children are afraid of their father. Whenever he is home they are always on their best behavior. Mrs. Hernandez often threatens the children by telling them that she will tell their father if they continue to misbehave. Mr. Hernandez uses corporal punishment as a means of disciplining the children. He has had one reported case of physical abuse toward Reuben, but the case was not substantiated because the marks were gone and Reuben did not admit that there had been marks.

Antonio Hernandez

Mr. Hernandez is a native of Puerto Rico. He is the oldest of two children. He has one brother who lives in Puerto Rico. Mr. Hernandez was raised in a very strict home environment. He grew up in a financially stable family. His father was a good provider. He was not very close to his father but feels that his father taught him a lot about taking care of a family. Mr. Hernandez is a strong-willed person who does not answer to anyone.

Andrea Hernandez

Mrs. Hernandez is an only child. She is a native of Costa Rica. She was raised with all the necessities of life. As a child, her father did not show her much affection because he was disappointed that she was not a boy. He had always wanted only one child and he prayed for a boy. Although he provided for her all of her life, their relationship was very distant. She was very close to her mother. Her mother overcompensated for the lack of attention from her father. She says her mother gave her everything she wanted. Mrs. Hernandez says growing up she was very quiet and somewhat passive. She says she spent her entire life trying to please her father. She desperately wanted him to be proud of her and love her.

Reuben

Reuben, 15 years old, is considered a leader among his peers. He is a very athletic child and is in a lot of extracurricular activities in school. He is an A student and is known as an overachiever. He works hard to please his father and is known as the peacemaker in the family. He secretly hopes that one day he will repay his father with the same kind of aggression with which he rules the house. He is angry that his mother allows his father to scream at her and to hit her. He has a female friend to whom he tells his problems, and she thinks he should call the police or ask his mother to leave his father. He knows his mother will never leave, and he is not sure they could make it without their father.

Sonia

Sonia is 10 years old and very shy, but she is a very good student. Her mother nurtures her. Sonia is very nervous and cannot tolerate a lot of noise. She loves school and has a good relationship with her teacher. Sonia's teacher has taken on a parental role in Sonia's life. Sonia often spends the night at her teacher's house. Sonia asked her mother if she could move in with her teacher, and her mother was very hurt at the thought that Sonia wanted to leave. Sonia does not interact well with others, as she is quiet and a loner. She enjoys being the teacher's helper. Her teacher has talked to Mrs. Hernandez about Sonia always feeling sad.

Rosa

Rosa is 5 years old and is truly the "baby of the family." She is Mr. Hernandez's favorite child. He displays a lot of affection toward her. Rosa is carefree and is pampered by the rest of the family. Rosa has just started kindergarten and she is excited because she gets to ride the school bus with her siblings.

She becomes afraid whenever she sees her father drinking and screaming. She generally hides in the closet until he calms down.

Extended Family

Mr. Hernandez's parents are Alcevedo and Patricia Hernandez. They were married in Puerto Rico and raised their children there. They moved to New York for business reasons; Mr. Hernandez was an import/export buyer for a large corporation. They are proud grandparents but maintain a distant relationship between themselves and their son. Patricia Hernandez says that Antonio was an angry child and has always had violent episodes. She says she has told her daughter-in-law never to upset him. Alcevedo and Patricia are close to their grandchildren.

Mrs. Hernandez's parents are Ricardo and Agustina Bennetti. They are afraid of Mr. Hernandez, and they do not visit the family often. They have encouraged their daughter to seek help and put a stop to the fights with her husband. The children have informed the maternal grandparents of the fights in the home between their mother and father.

SAFETY AND RISK ASSESSMENT QUESTIONS

1. What form of abuse is present in this family?

2. What are the specific injuries to the child or children?

3. How do these injuries determine intervention?

4. How does the abuse impact protection of the child or children in the home?

5. Does the abuse impact family preservation? Explain.

6. What cultural factors must be considered in the determination of what constitutes emotional or verbal abuse?

7. How do these factors impact your perception or ability to work with this family?

8. How does your definition or perception of emotional and/or verbal abuse contribute to your assessment?

FAMILY CASE ANALYSIS—ENGAGEMENT

1. What is the presenting problem? How are the family members involved in the situation defining the problem?

2. In exploring the situation, how does the information that you learn from other family members inform your perceptions?

3. How would you define the working problem based on the current information?

4. What strategies do you think would be useful in engaging with the individuals involved?

FAMILY ASSESSMENT

1. How would your definition of the working problem direct your assessment?

2. What assumptions about human and social behavior are you making, and how would you follow up with these?

3. Are there other problems or issues you think might emerge as you delve deeper into this case? What are they, and how might they affect the situation?

4. What information are you lacking about the situation and its context that you feel you need to know to gain an in-depth understanding?

5. Identify the strengths, limitations, and barriers present in this family. Based on the strengths, where would you start to work with this family?

6. What issues of motivation and/or resistance do you think you are likely to encounter? How do you think you might handle them?

7. Give a clear and concise summary of your assessment, and state how it affects the defining of general goals.

8. Identify and briefly state at least two theoretical frameworks or approaches that would guide your intervention in working with this family.

9. Prepare a genogram and an ecomap for the family, using the blanks given as Figures 4.1 and 4.2.

PLANNING FOR THE FAMILY

1. State your general goals in working with this family.

2. State specific objectives related to each goal, and identify specific changes in the situation that might lead to accomplishing the above goals.

3. What actions should be taken by the worker, the clients, or others to operationalize your objectives?

4. How are you going to set up your evaluation to track accomplishments or progress in goals and objectives? (*Note:* This section should reflect knowledge of methods of practice evaluation.)

The _____ Family

Male ▼ Pregnancy – – – Marital separation ? Whereabouts unknown
Female ×× Death ·····/·/···· Divorce

FIGURE 4.1   The Family Genogram
(Sketch a genogram of the facts of this family structure.)

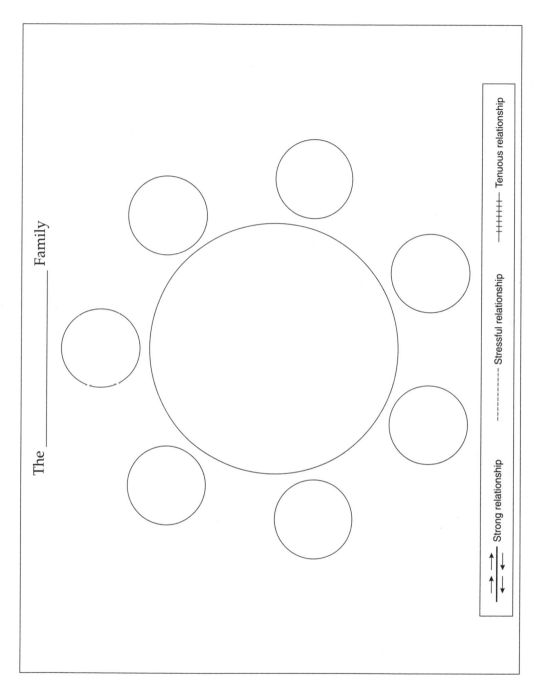

FIGURE 4.2   The Family Ecomap

FAMILY TREATMENT PLAN/CONTRACT

Design a treatment plan for this family. This is an example of a treatment/contract plan. Most practice texts provide examples.

The Brown Family Treatment/Contract Plan

Client: _____ (Define the client here.)

I. **Brief Description of the Problem**
(This is generally a summary of the reasons the client came to you or your agency.)

II. **Primary Goals and Objectives** (Find a format that is clear to your client and you.)

    1. Goal:

            Objective:

    2. Goal:

            Objective:

    3. Goal:

            Objective:

III. **We, the undersigned, agree to the following tasks:**

    1.

    2.

IV. **Evaluation of Progress** (How your plan will be evaluated.)

_____

_____   _____

                                      Signature of Social Worker

_____

Signature(s) of Client(s)

_____   _____

(Date)   (Date)

SUGGESTED READINGS

Davies, L., & Rains, P. (1995). Single mothers by choice. *Families in Society, 76*(9), 543–550.

Debaryshe, B. D. (1998). A developmental perspective on anger: Family and peer contexts. *Psychology in the Schools, 35*(3), 205–227.

DeYoung, M. (1998). Another look at moral panics: The case of satanic day care centers. *Deviant Behavior, 19*(3), 257–278.

Dore, M. M., Nelson-Zluplo, L., & Kaufmann, E. (1999). Friends in need: Designing and implementing a psychoeducational group for school children from drug-involved families. *Social Work, 44*(2), 179–190.

Douglass, A. (1996). Rethinking the effects of homelessness on children: Resiliency and competency. *Child Welfare, 75*(6), 741–751.

Dyson, L. L. (1998). A support program for siblings of children with disabilities: What siblings learn and what they like. *Psychology in the Schools, 35*(1), 57–65.

Forte, J. A., Franks, D. D., & Rigsby, D. (1996). Asymmetrical role-taking: Comparing battered and nonbattered women. *Social Work, 41*(1), 59–73.

Fraser, M. W., Nelson, K. E., & Rivard, J. C. (1997). Effectiveness of family preservation services. *Social Work Research, 21*(4), 138–153.

Gardner, H. (1996). The concept of family: Perceptions of children in family foster care. *Child Welfare, 75*(2), 161–182.

Gupta, G. R. (1996). AIDS and the new orphans: Coping with death. *Journal of Comparative Family Studies, 27*(3), 582–584.

Hairston, C. F. (1998). The forgotten parent: Understanding the forces that influence incarcerate fathers' relationships with their children. *Child Welfare, 77*(5), 617–639.

Hay, I., Ashman, A. F., & Van Kraayenoord, C. E. (1998). Educational characteristics of students with high or low self-concept. *Psychology in the Schools, 35*(4), 391–400.

Lichtenstein, T. (1995). To tell or not to tell: Factors affecting adoptees' telling their adoptive parents about their search. *Child Welfare, 75*(1), 61–72.

O'Keefe, M. (1996). The differential effects of family violence on adolescent adjustment. *Child and Adolescent Social Work Journal, 13*(1): 51–68.

Ringwalt, C. L., Greene, J. M., Robertson, M., & McPheeters, M. (1998). The prevalence of homelessness among adolescents in the United States. *American Journal of Public Health, 88*(9), 1325–1329.

Rose, S. J., & Meezan, W. (1996). Variations in perceptions of child neglect. *Child Welfare, 75*(2), 139–160.

Strein, W., Simonson, T., & Vail, L. (1999). Convergence of views: Self-perceptions of African Americans and white kindergartners. *Psychology in the Schools, 36*(2), 125–134.

Vissing, Y. M., & Diament, J. (1997). Housing distress among high school students. *Social Work, 42*(1), 31–41.

Volling, B. L., Youngblade, L. M., & Belesky, J. (1997). Young children's social relationships with siblings and friends. *American Journal of Orthopsychiatry, 67*(1), 102–111.

White, J. (1997). *Weeding out the Tears.* New York: Avon.

White, R. (1991). *Ryan White: My Own Story.* New York: Penguin.

Wilhelmus, M. (1998). Mediation in kinship care: Another step in the provision of culturally relevant child welfare services. *Social Work, 43*(2), 117–126.

Zuravin, S. J., & DePanfilis, D. (1997). Factors affecting foster care placement of children receiving child protective services. *Social Work Research, 21*(1), 34–42.

CHAPTER FIVE

SEXUAL ABUSE

THE ABERNATHY FAMILY

Student Instructions

You are working as a foster care worker in a state child welfare agency. You have just been assigned to work with the Abernathy family. The purpose of your involvement is to ensure that the family attends counseling and that the children are safe. The state currently has legal custody of the Abernathy children, but the mother still has physical custody. The Abernathy family is involved in a family counseling program designed to work with families in which sexual abuse has occurred. The program provides therapy for the entire family. There is an adolescent group, individual therapy, family therapy, and a sex offenders group. The Abernathy family has gone through a difficult ordeal. Mr. Abernathy was arrested and charged with child molestation. The court will evaluate the family situation in eight months and decide whether Mr. Abernathy will serve jail time. If he completes treatment, the judge will consider probation.

The family misses Mr. Abernathy very much, and everyone wants him back home. Mrs. Abernathy does not want the community or their friends to find out exactly what has happened. She is threatening to stop your involvement and possibly run away with the children, because she says they "will work things out together" and feels that you are asking too many questions about the family. She is upset with her husband, Phillip, and her daughter, Melanie, and wonders what made them do this to her. She states that she loves her children and has given them the best in life. The judge issued a court order stating that Mr. Abernathy cannot have any contact with his daughters. If he violates the court order, he will have to go to jail. Your job is to ensure the safety of the girls and make sure that the family continues treatment. Your final report will determine the disposition of the case, and your report will be used in court.

Family Composition

The Abernathy family consists of the parents, Phillip, age 39, and Nancy, age 37. They have two adopted children, Melanie, age 15, and Patricia, age 11. This family is very close to their extended family. Mrs. Betsy Davis is Mrs. Abernathy's mother, and she lives nearby; Mrs. Veronica Lewis and Mr. Vernon Abernathy are Mr. Abernathy's siblings. They are all involved in the family. Vernon Abernathy lives about a thousand miles away, but he does communicate with them on a monthly basis.

Current Situation

About a month ago, Melanie told a friend that her father was having sexual intercourse with her. She begged her friend not to tell anyone and told her this was a secret. Her friend was so upset about the situation that she told the school social worker. The social worker contacted the Department of Children and Family Services (DCFS) and the police department. The sexual abuse was confirmed. Mr. Abernathy was arrested, and Melanie and her sister, Patricia, were taken into legal custody by the state, but left in the physical custody of their mother. The family was referred to counseling, and the case was to remain open for supervision by the foster care unit. Mr. Abernathy was released from jail on a $50,000 bond after two weeks and ordered to go to counseling, and is now staying with his sister. Melanie is glad that she disclosed the sexual abuse, but feels responsible for the breakup of the family. Melanie's younger sister, Patricia, is very angry at the entire family; she will not interact in treatment, and cries all the time.

Family Background

The Abernathy family is a Caucasian family living in a middle-class neighborhood. Their annual income is about $85,000 a year. The parents have been married for eighteen years. According to Mrs. Abernathy, as a result of this recent situation, she feels their marriage might not survive. She states that they do not communicate the way they used to, and Mr. Abernathy is not even interested in being intimate with her.

Phillip Abernathy

Mr. Abernathy is the oldest of three children. He describes his childhood as a "nightmare." He says his mother was a loving and supportive mother. He describes his mother as a very passive person but states that she loved them with all of her heart. He says his father was a rigid, mean, controlling, and abusive man. He remembers always trying to do things that might make his father proud of him. He states that he does not remember his father ever praising him for anything. His father did not allow the children to socialize with other people or participate in any after-school activities. He states that his mother secretly allowed him to participate in programs at school. He says his mother took a lot of abuse for loving and paying attention to her children. He always wondered why his mother did not leave his father. He says they were all afraid of his father, and his mother would instruct them to keep quiet and never upset him.

Mr. Abernathy says his father never wanted children, but agreed to allow his mother to have children as long as she did not require him to help her raise them. He says his father spent most of his time pretending that they did not exist. He says his father always reminded them that he did not want them. He remembers his father telling his mother to come and watch television but would tell her "your children are not allowed in my living room." He says they never ate meals together or did family activities. Mr. Abernathy says that one of the saddest days of his life was when his mother went into the hospital to have his brother, Vernon. He says his father never went to the hospital and would not allow his mother to bring Vernon home from the hospital. He says Vernon had to go and live with his mother's sister, Joanna. He says they all cried and his father did not speak to any of them for weeks. He says that his mother would take them to see Vernon, and he and his sister would wish that they could live with Vernon and their Aunt Joanna. He says his Aunt Joanna was very good to them and she would buy them things and sneak money to his mother to care for them. He says his aunt always bought their school clothes. He stated that after Vernon went to live with his aunt, his mother went into a deep depression and it took everything in her to care for them. He says his mother did not work because his father told her she did not need any money. He remembers his mother wanting to work so she could take better care of them as children.

Mr. Abernathy says that when he was 3 years old his father made him take baths with him and would lock the bathroom door so his mother would not come in. He says he does not remember what happened in the bathroom with his father, but he does remember crying and being really sad. He says his mother always begged his father not to hurt him. He says there were times when his father would say, "I am going to teach you how to be a man." He says his father would take him away from home and make him sit on his lap in the car and would tell him that he was teaching him to drive. Mr. Abernathy states that when he was 10, his father told his mother that he was taking him hunting—only they did not hunt. He says his father "hurt" him and put a gun to his head and told him, "You better never remember what happened here." He says he vowed that he would never remember what happened.

Mr. Abernathy says that when he was 17 years old and a senior in high school, his father died of lung cancer. He says his father smoked a lot. He says that his father was not sick a long time—he died three months after he was diagnosed with cancer. He remembers vividly the day his father died, because it was the happiest day of their lives. He says none of them cried at his father's funeral. He thought his mother would cry, but she did not. He says that two days after his father was buried his mother woke them up and told them, "We are moving out of this prison." He says his mother spent one week packing all of their belongings and they moved into one of his aunt's houses. He says his mother left all of his father's things. They did not take anything that belonged to him. He says his mother never said anything bad about his father.

Mr. Abernathy states that he graduated from high school six months after his father died and he decided to go to college in the same town. His mother needed him because there was no income coming into the house. In his junior year, he met Nancy and they were married. When he finished college, he got a job with a major firm as an architect. He has been very faithful to his job for eighteen years.

He says that he and his wife never had problems until they adopted their children. He says they tried to have children but were unsuccessful. He feels that after they adopted Melanie things changed in their relationship, and his wife did not have time for him anymore. He says that they spent very little time together. He decided two years ago he should become more involved in Melanie's life. He says Melanie is a happy girl and full of life. He states that he is really turned on by her personality. He says until five years ago he left caring for the children up to his wife, and she complained that the children needed more of his time. He says that in the last two years Melanie has made him forget about working so much. He loves being with her and she makes him feel young. He denies having sex with his daughter, but admits "playing around" on occasions. He says he is happy that she told someone, because it might have gone further. He goes to trial in eight months and is concerned about what will happen to his family. He is currently living with his sister, Veronica Lewis, who is very close to him. She, however, is angry because she cannot believe he would do such a thing. He has to attend a sex offenders group regularly. He does not understand why, because he feels he is not like those other men. He is extremely embarrassed about all of this and says that it will never happen again. He struggles with having to keep talking about it.

Nancy Abernathy

Mrs. Abernathy is the middle child of three children: she has two brothers. She has always been very independent and is seen by her family as a "caretaker." She describes her childhood as a lot of fun. Her family spent a lot of time together, and she always wanted a family so that she could continue the tradition of doing some of the things that they started. She states that she is close to both of her parents. Her parents were not in favor of her marrying Mr. Abernathy, but they have always been supportive of her choices. She says when she met her husband in college he was goal-oriented and a very quiet man. She says he was loving and always told her how much he appreciated the relationship she had with her family. She says they graduated from college the same year and he got a job as an architect and she got a job as a registered nurse. She says that she had to teach her husband how to be a "family man" because his family was not close. She states that it is hard to believe he would violate his own child. She remembers him making little comments about young girls after they got married, but never thought he would act on them with his own child. She states that she is very hurt that he would do such a crazy thing and mess up everything they have worked for. She says he cannot come home right now, but she hopes their family will be together again soon. She feels that he has learned the lesson that this was inappropriate and that maybe they do not need counseling because they can work this out themselves.

Melanie

Melanie is 15 years old and very smart academically. She says she is very close to her father but has a closer relationship with her mother, as her mother does everything with them. She says her father is nice but does not spend much time with them. She says he is quiet and likes to be alone. She says he does not like to be affectionate. Melanie states that in the last two years her father has become more involved in her school activities, taking her to cheerleading practice and sometimes to after-school functions such as basketball games. She says her mother is not a sports person, but her father loves sports. She says all of the girls on the cheerleading squad love her father, as he always takes them out to eat after practice and buys them gifts.

Melanie states that he has been acting "weird" lately and telling sexual jokes to her; she has said, "Don't say those things, Dad." She says in the last few months she has not wanted him to take her to practice or pick her up. She says that on a couple of occasions he touched her and told her he was playing and for her not to say anything about it. She says she was afraid to tell her mother. However, one day after cheerleading practice, she told her best friend that her father was having sex with her. Now, she feels her family has been destroyed as a result of it. She wishes she had kept it a secret. She is having a difficult time concentrating on her school work, and she cannot eat, and she wishes she was dead. She wants to see her father and apologize for what she has done, but the court said he cannot have any contact with them until he completes sex offenders' treatment. She did not tell anyone exactly what he did. She says she is not afraid of him and misses him very much. She states that he was a good father.

Patricia

Patricia is 11 years old and very happy. She laughs all the time and is very close to her father. The family thinks she does not know what has happened. She acts as if she does not. She says when the social worker and police interviewed Melanie, they asked her if her father had "hurt" her and she says she told them "no." She says she does know some things, but nobody has asked her any detailed questions. She wants her father home and blames her sister for everything. She is refusing to talk to her sister and is upset that they have to go to counseling. She has been very sad since he left, and she wonders when he will be allowed to return home.

Betsy Davis

Betsy Davis, age 59, is Mrs. Abernathy's mother. Her husband died two years ago, and she has had to make a big adjustment to life without him. She now lives about an hour away from her daughter. She cannot believe this is happening and says they have just the "perfect" family. She feels that maybe her granddaughter is making this up to get attention. She states that she has been proud to have Mr. Abernathy as a son-in-law. She thinks that when young girls get to a certain age, they start to dream about this kind of stuff. She would like for the girls to come and stay with her until "this all blows over." She feels that her daughter needs some time with her husband to work all of this out. She told her daughter that they should not attend counseling, because then everyone will know their business. She says she and her husband raised their daughter to be very private and maintain a good image in the community. She says that maybe adoption was not a good idea. She also feels that maybe Melanie's biological family had some kind of problem and it is now beginning to show up. She always felt that Melanie might have come from a "bad seed," because she was "very friendly and loved to lay all over men." She says that she could remember when Melanie was only 5 and she displayed certain behaviors. She is wondering if Patricia might go through the same ordeal when she gets to be Melanie's age.

Veronica Lewis

Veronica Lewis, age 36, is Mr. Abernathy's sister. According to her, she and her brother are very close and she is having a difficult time with this situation. She is constantly wondering "why" or "what" would cause her brother to do such a thing. According to Ms. Lewis, they were not raised this way. She says their childhood was horrible, but they were not violated in any way. She says that their father was abusive and meaner to Phillip, but they made it through all of that. She says she has developed a love for the girls but has always been against adoption, because she says who knows where "these people" come from. Ms. Lewis never had children herself and is now glad that she never considered adoption. She has seen the children only once since all of this happened, and she was not allowed to ask them any questions about the situation. She feels that if she could just talk to Melanie, then they could work this out and she could make her "stop this nonsense." She is embarrassed and confused. On the other hand, she has a close relationship with Melanie and thinks maybe Melanie is telling the truth. She says Melanie is not a child who would lie. She feels she needs to support her brother, as he has no place else to go. She says that when their mother died a year ago, she told them to take care of each other. She really does not know what to do or what to believe. She is not very close to her younger brother, Vernon, but she does talk to him on a monthly basis. He lives about a thousand miles from them.

Vernon Abernathy

Vernon is 30 years old and lives on the West Coast with his wife and four daughters. He says that he had a wonderful childhood. He says it was nice having two mothers, although he never understood why he could not live with his siblings. He says his aunt always told him that she was his aunt and not his mother. He says he would call her "Mom" anyway and call his real mother "Mother." He is somewhat close to his siblings but was not raised with them until he was 9 years old. He says by the time he got into high school, Phillip was leaving home. He says he was not allowed to live with them, but no one ever told him why. He states that he sort of figured things out because he did not see his father for the first time until he was 5 years old, and his father never spoke to him. He says his mother and aunt always made him feel special. He says he did not attend his father's funeral because he was in school and his mother did not want to take him out of school for the ceremony. He says he cannot believe this is happening to his brother, because he does not remember hearing anything about his brother being abused. He says that he has allowed his daughters to spend two weeks with his brother's children in the summer. He does not think anything has happened to his daughters. He says he does not know how to respond to this situation or what to do.

THE HALLMARK FAMILY

Student Instructions

You are a social worker in a private child welfare agency. Your agency counsels families that come to the attention of the state Department of Children and Family Services (DCFS). The department investigated the case of 12-year-old Vanessa: it was alleged that something sexual happened between her and her uncle, who also resides in the home. When the investigator went to talk to Vanessa, she did not disclose exactly what happened to her. However, she did disclose that something had happened between her and her uncle. Vanessa's family was asked to move out of the home for her safety until the case could be further investigated. The department has decided to keep the case open while the child attends counseling at your agency, in hopes that the child will disclose more information to you. You are a mandated reporter, and are required to report anything the child discloses to you to DCFS. The family has also asked to be seen by your agency. You are just seeing the child; another therapist in your office is seeing the rest of the family.

Family Composition

The Hallmark family consists of the parents, Daniel, age 32, and Joanne, age 31. They have two children, a daughter, Vanessa, age 12, and a son, Bernie, age 6. They reside in the home with Mr. Hallmark's brother, Eddie, age 35, and his wife, Mimi, age 33.

Current Situation

In your third session with Vanessa she disclosed that her uncle Eddie had sex with her. Specifically, she stated that he had oral sex with her on several occasions. She has also told you that other things have happened, but she is afraid to tell you anything else for fear it might hurt her uncle more. Eddie was arrested two days ago after Vanessa disclosed the oral sex in counseling. He has no bond, and everyone in the family is upset. Daniel is angry and confused about the whole situation. Joanne and Mimi do not know what to do and are comforting each other. Mimi thinks that maybe Eddie had a breakdown and is now "crazy." The family is in disarray and no one knows exactly what to do.

Family Background

Daniel and Joanne have been married for thirteen years. They reside in a nice small home in a working-class neighborhood in a metropolitan city. They have a yearly income of $50,000. Daniel and Joanne met in high school and fell in love. They decided that they would get married after they graduated. One week after graduation they were married, and they worked all summer in order to get their own place and have money for college. When August came they had just enough money to pay their college tuition but not enough to get their own apartment. They moved in with Daniel's brother, Eddie, and his wife, Mimi. After their first year in college, Joanne got pregnant but was determined not to drop out of college. After Vanessa was born, Mimi agreed to babysit Vanessa. Mimi is very close to Vanessa and at times has had to detach when Joanne comes home because Vanessa calls both of them "Mom." Daniel and Joanne have lived with Eddie and Mimi since their first year in college. They decided to stay even after Daniel finished college, because Vanessa was so attached to Mimi. Mimi and Eddie are like Vanessa's second parents. The family relies totally on Daniel and Joanne's income.

In the last three months Vanessa has been clingy toward Joanne and distant from Mimi and Eddie. Mimi has asked Vanessa what is wrong, but she has "shut down" and will not talk to her. At times she goes to Mimi and hugs her, but she will not say anything. She wants to go everywhere with Joanne and Joanne has also asked Vanessa, "What is the matter?" Vanessa jokes and says, "I just want to be with you, Mama." Vanessa is extremely distant from Eddie. Eddie always took her to after-school activities and now she does not want him anywhere around her. He does not push her but is acting like he has no clue what the problems are.

Daniel Hallmark

Daniel is a Caucasian male. He has a college degree in accounting and is employed by a small accounting firm. He is the middle child of three children. His father is deceased and his mother has Alzheimer's disease. She lives in a nursing home in the same town. His younger sister resides in a women's home in Colorado. She was born a quadriplegic. She was placed in a home after their father died ten years ago. Daniel is very close to Eddie. Eddie always looked out for Daniel.

Joanne Hallmark

Joanne is Caucasian and Asian. Her father was German and her mother was Vietnamese. Her parents met when her father was in the military and stationed in Vietnam. She attended college with Daniel, but because of financial reasons never finished her degree. She has vowed to go back and finish. She is employed at the local elementary school as a paraprofessional. She has no siblings. Her parents live in Alaska, so she rarely sees them. Six years after Vanessa was born, Joanne had a baby boy named Bernie. After Bernie was born, Joanne stayed home from work for six months to bond with him because she remembers how difficult her relationship was with Vanessa. She and Bernie are very close. Joanne has always felt sort of guilty about her relationship with Vanessa and not being there in her early development years. However, she is close to Mimi and has appreciated her being there to care for Vanessa in the home. Joanne was born in the United States and Mimi was born in Vietnam. Mimi shares so much culture with Joanne that Joanne likewise has been a support to her. They consider each other almost sisters.

Vanessa

Vanessa is 12 years old with brown eyes and long dark hair. She is very friendly and gregarious. Vanessa has always been a fairly confident little girl, and people often compliment her on her attitude and zest for life. She is very outgoing and loves to be the center of attention. She loves school and is an average student. She is in the yearbook club and on the drama team.

Approximately four months ago, Vanessa became withdrawn. She started wanting to spend the night with friends and did not want to come home. Mimi and Joanne spoke to her, but Vanessa just said that she wanted to live with her friends. Joanne thought it was a phase and overlooked it. However, Mimi was very concerned and started to spend more time with Vanessa. Vanessa asked Mimi, "What if someone we know did something to me, what would you do?" Mimi assured her that she would always protect her. One Friday after school, Eddie picked Vanessa up and took her to the movies and shopping. When Vanessa came home, she was very sad and Mimi asked her if she had a good time. Vanessa nodded and said "yes," but went to her room. Mimi asked Eddie what happened, and he stated that when he picked her up from school she appeared upset. Later that night Joanne talked to Vanessa and found her in her room crying. Vanessa said only that she did not want to see Eddie again. Joanne asked why, but Vanessa said nothing. The family talked about it without Vanessa present, and they all agreed to try and find out what was wrong. Later, Vanessa confided in Mimi that Eddie had hurt her, but she would not say what he had done. Mimi was upset and confronted Eddie, and he denied that he and Vanessa had a problem. He says he told her she could not have something that she wanted in the mall. Mimi took his word but felt something was wrong, because they have told Vanessa "no" before and she did not get upset.

The next day, Vanessa went to spend the night with her best friend, Brenda. She told Brenda that she was angry at Eddie and then started to cry. Brenda did not know what was wrong with Vanessa other than she told her that she hated Eddie. Brenda told her mother and father and they talked to Vanessa. Vanessa revealed to them only that Eddie had hurt her but did not tell them how he hurt her. When they offered to call Vanessa's family, Vanessa pleaded with them not to tell that she had confided in them. So they did not tell her family, but the next day Brenda's mother called the Child Protective Services hotline and asked some questions. She was convinced to make a report.

Bernie

Bernie is 6 years old and basically very happy. He is in the first grade at the local elementary school where Joanne works. He goes to work with her every day. Bernie has a close relationship with his parents. He loves Vanessa and always seeks her approval. Bernie has been in day care since he was about a year old. Mimi kept him for about six months after Joanne went back to work. However, he is not close to Mimi, and Joanne made sure that he bonded with her. Bernie is not aware of what is going on but now feels a little neglected by Joanne.

Eddie Hallmark

Eddie is a 35-year-old blue-collar worker. He never went to college, but he supported Daniel financially while he was in college. Eddie was in the military for eight years and was stationed in Vietnam for five years. He met Mimi in Vietnam and married her there. After leaving the military, he got a job working with a major airline. He lost his job about five months ago, after working for that company for ten years, partly because of his clinical depression. He has battled depression since he left the military. His employer asked him to get counseling but he refuses. He was given warnings about his temper. Recently he got into a fight with a co-worker and was suspended from his job. When he went back to work after his suspension, he threatened to kill his co-worker, so he was fired. Although he says he was angry, he says that he would never hurt anyone. Eddie has always been a responsible man but as a child felt neglected by his parents and never felt loved by his father. He remembers not being very close to his father and always being protective of Daniel.

Mimi Hallmark

Mimi is a 33-year-old Vietnamese woman. She is fairly quiet but a very loving woman. She met Eddie while he was in the military in Vietnam, married him there, and returned to the United States with him. She has three older brothers and no sisters. Her family still lives in Vietnam. Recently she lost her father to cancer. Her mother is still living in the family home. She has returned to Vietnam only once since she left, and that was for her father's funeral. She would love to return home more often, but financially they cannot afford it. She does not work but has wanted to work. However, Eddie never wanted her to work, and when Vanessa was born, Joanne and Daniel asked her to care for Vanessa. This was a joy for her, because three years after she was married she learned that she could not have children. For about six years she went to many doctors and tried everything to have a child, but she was unsuccessful. According to Mimi, caring for Vanessa saved her life. She is very close to Vanessa and thinks of her as her own daughter. She has taught Vanessa to speak her language and although she is not fluent, Vanessa recognizes words and phrases. Mimi states that her marriage is "good" but that Eddie has had problems and is often depressed. She is not sure why, but says she tries to make him happy. She is very happy that Joanne and Daniel moved in with them and considers Joanne her sister.

She felt Eddie had done something to Vanessa but did not know what. She was devastated to learn that Eddie would touch Vanessa in a sexual way. She stated to Eddie, "She is like your daughter." Although Mimi does not think Vanessa is lying, she does not know why Eddie would do such a thing. Mimi has been in the United States for more than ten years, but she has little exposure to the world outside of her family. Mimi says that Eddie is not abusive to her and she has never seen him be abusive to anyone in the home. Mimi is afraid that they will all be split up and does not know what will happen to her. She has no money or resources to help Eddie. Mimi does not drive and feels afraid to ask Joanne and Daniel to take her to visit Eddie. She is feeling very alone now.

THE WEBSTER FAMILY

Student Instructions

You are a protective services worker with the Department of Children and Family Services (DCFS). You received a call from the local elementary school regarding possible sexual abuse of Julian Webster, an 11-year-old female. You visited the school and interviewed Julian. She disclosed sexual abuse and, based on what she told you, you must take her into protective custody and investigate the case further. You will have to decide if Callie or Cynthia has been abused as well, determine placement of the girls, and make an assessment of the situation.

Family Composition

The Webster family household consists of Mervin, age 32, and his wife, Felicia Cooper-Webster, age 33. Mervin has two daughters, Callie, age 13, and Julian, age 11. Felicia has one daughter, Cynthia Cooper, age 9. All three girls reside in the home. Kirsten Webster, age 31, is the biological mother of Callie and Julian. She does not live in the home, but she is very involved in her daughters' lives.

Current Situation

Julian Webster has just been taken into protective custody and placed in a foster home. Julian lives with her father, her stepmother, and her sisters, Callie and Cynthia. Mr. Webster is in the process of being charged with aggravated child molestation. Julian and Callie's biological mother lives in another city and is not aware of the whole situation. The stepmother is very confused and does not know whom to believe. She thinks this is a nightmare, and she is hysterical and emotionally out of control. She is refusing to call the biological mother and does not want her involved. No one has interviewed Callie or Cynthia yet, although the police suspect that she might have been abused as well.

During your interview with Julian, age 11, she disclosed the following to you. On Wednesday, after she returned from a visit to her mother's home for the summer, her father made her get on the sofa in the living room and he forced her to suck on his penis. He ejaculated in her mouth and made her swallow his semen. He told her that Wednesdays were good days for him and that they would be bad days for her. The next Wednesday, when she got home from school, he made her take off her clothes and put on her stepmother's see-through pink nightgown. On his bed, he forced open her mouth and made her suck his penis again. He then told her to scream "F— me, baby." She did what he said and he penetrated her vagina with his penis. He then pulled it out of her and forced her to suck his penis until he ejaculated in her mouth. She spit it out. He told her he thought she liked it and that she was just playing hard to get. He also told her that she was beginning to look just like her mother and that is why he enjoyed making love to her. He also told her never to tell anyone or she would have to go to court and he would have to go to jail and people would hate her for telling on her father. The next Wednesday, when she got home from school, he made her go into the dining room and forced her to suck his penis.

Family Background

The Webster family is an upper-middle-class family and reside in the suburbs of a large metropolitan area. The family income is approximately $125,000 per year. Mr. Webster is an engineer and his wife, Felicia, is a bookkeeper for a major accounting firm. When Mr. Webster divorced his first wife, Kirsten, he fought her for custody of the children. The judge granted him custody because he appeared to be the more stable at the time. Julian and Callie came to live with him when they were 10 and 8, respectively. Until that time they had lived with both parents. They spent summers with their mother. Mr. Webster married Felicia one year after he divorced Kirsten. Felicia has one child, Cynthia, who is 9 years old. Felicia is not very close to her stepdaughters, and she feels that Mr. Webster is too close to them. Julian has heard her on the phone telling her friends, "I can't stand Julian; you would think that she is Mervin's woman instead of me." Julian has never told anyone in the family what has happened to her.

Mervin Webster

Mervin Webster is a 32-year-old African American. He grew up in a house with two older brothers, Blain and Rocky, and two younger sisters, Karen and Sylvia. Blain has one son, Rocky has one daughter, Karen has three girls and one boy, and Sylvia has one daughter. According to his mother, he was a very "weird " boy growing up. She states that he was involved in Boy Scouts and all kinds of activities. He says he never liked his mother because she was too controlling. He seemed to get along better with his sisters and was always bossing them around. He states that he is not really close to any of his siblings and that his sisters refuse to talk to him and he does not know why. He also states that he would love for his girls to get to know their cousins, but every time he invites his nieces to his house, they never show up. Mr. Webster does not have many friends, and he says he considers himself a "family man."

Felicia Cooper-Webster

Mrs. Webster is an African-American woman who has been married to Mr. Webster for two-and-a-half years. She states that they are very happy. She says she married him because it was obvious that he was a "family man." She also states he did not hang out in the streets with his friends. In fact, he had very few friends. She says that he seemed to be a good father to his girls and that was what she wanted for her daughter. She liked that about him, because her last husband, who was Cynthia's father, was so distant and spent too much time with his friends. She says she only has one problem with her marriage and that is that Mr. Webster wants the girls to do everything with them. She says that sometimes she does not mind, but the girls like to be alone sometimes. Also, she would like some private time with him. She says it has been a long time since they have been intimate.

Callie

Callie is a very outgoing 13-year-old. She hates her father but has learned to get along with him. She is constantly asking to spend the night with her friends, and in the last year he has let her. She says that he used to give her a lot of attention, but lately he ignores her and it makes her mad. She states that sometimes he acts as if she does not exist. She says that he is always giving in to Julian and that she and Julian hardly ever talk anymore. Callie says that six months ago, after she had been asking for her own room, her father gave Julian her own room. Callie had to share a room with Cynthia. She says she wishes they could live with their mom, but that her father would never hear of it. She says they cry when it is time to come home after the summer. However, their mother has told them that their father can take better care of them financially.

Julian

Julian is a very bright and outgoing 11-year-old. She has a beautiful smile. Julian has dark black hair, and her eyes are gray. Her father has told her on several occasions that she looks exactly like her mother. Julian is very close to one of her teachers but does not feel comfortable enough to disclose her situation, because she does not want her teacher to think badly of her. The teacher does, however, sense that something is wrong with Julian. One day in class the teacher gave everyone a questionnaire and asked all of the students to tell her something about themselves. In the "other" section of the questionnaire Julian wrote, "What if one of your parents was doing something to you that you thought was wrong, what could you do?" After Julian wrote this question, she erased it. However, the teacher was still able to read the question. After class the teacher asked Julian if she could speak with her. That is when Julian disclosed that she was being "touched in the wrong way" by her father. Julian is very ashamed of what has been going on but says she feels good that maybe someone could talk to her father and get him to stop.

Kirsten Webster

Kirsten is the biological mother of Callie and Julian. She lives in Miami, Florida. She moved there after she and Mervin separated. Shortly after she moved, they were divorced and he won full custody of the children because she had had a "nervous breakdown." She and Mervin were married for eight years, and they had a very abusive marriage. According to her, Mervin was abusive to her and after five years of their marriage she had her first nervous breakdown and he convinced her that she could not care for her children. During their marriage she was a housewife and she felt that she was a good mother. Both girls are very close to her and have often asked to live with her. However, Mervin told her that if she ever tried to get custody of the girls, he would kill her. She wanted the girls to come live with her but felt that they were better off financially by living with their father. Since their divorce she has finished junior college in computer science and has a very good job. She is devastated about what has happened to the girls and blames herself. She is not sure she can care for them, since she had two "nervous breakdowns" and was later diagnosed with manic depression (bipolar disorder). She would like to try to bring them to live with her, but Mervin has told her that he will kill her and she believes him. She is not sure what to do, but she wants to provide for her daughters.

THE VASQUEZ FAMILY

Student Instructions

You are a hospital pediatric social worker and the police have just brought a mother and her two children to the hospital. The mother is hysterical, and no one seems to be able to control her. She is crying and screaming that her husband has molested her daughter. Her daughter appears okay and is not crying but is clinging to her mother. The police woke the children up when they arrived. The mother does not want the child examined, even though she has told the police and you that the child has been molested. She says her husband left the house and his whereabouts are unknown. You will need to interview the mother and the child to determine what happened, and then make an assessment of the situation. You are also required by law to report this allegation to the Department of Children and Family Services (DCFS).

Family Composition

The Vasquez family consists of the parents, Alvin, age 38, and his wife, Melinda, age 26. They have two children, Alvin, Jr., age 5, and Sarah, age 3.

The extended family is involved with this family. The maternal grandparents live next door, and Mr. Vasquez's two older sisters live a few blocks away.

Current Situation

Alvin Vasquez and his wife, Melinda Perez-Vasquez, had a domestic dispute after Mrs. Vasquez attacked him when he returned from work. She told him that he had molested their 3-year-old daughter, Sarah. They fought physically in the house, and Mr. Vasquez left the home. Mr. Vasquez sustained a large cut over his right eye and a broken finger. Mrs. Vasquez sustained a cut lip and a black eye. When Mr. Vasquez left the house, Mrs. Vasquez called the police. After Mrs. Vasquez called the police, she locked the children in the house and went to look for Mr. Vasquez. When the police arrived, no adult was at home. The police then received a call stating that a woman two blocks over appeared lost and was crying and calling for her husband. The police went to the location and the woman identified herself as Melinda Vasquez. She told the police she was looking for her husband. The police took Melinda back to her house to get the children. They then transported her and the two children to the hospital. Mr. Vasquez showed up at the police station with his two sisters to give a report about the incident. He was bleeding and appeared somewhat hysterical.

According to Mr. Vasquez, when he got home from work, his wife was pacing the floor, screaming profanity in English and Spanish, and crying. He says he approached her to try and calm her down, and she started beating him about the face and head. He states that he tried to restrain her and keep her under control, but she was like a "crazy woman." He says he tried to call the police and she snatched the phone cord out of the wall. He also tried to leave the house to get help, and she took the car keys. He said he then decided just to leave and walk to his sister's house for help. He says the children were in their room and appeared to be sleep. He states that about every three months his wife acts "bizarre." He has asked her to see a doctor, but she refuses. He says he has had to leave home on several occasions for the same reason, and it appears that she is getting worse. He says he does not know what to do. He states that he does not like to leave the children when she is upset, but she has never hurt her children. He states that he would never sexually abuse anyone, especially his own child. He states that she has accused him of sexually molesting their daughter before. The first time she accused him was when they lived in Texas and their daughter was 2 months old. He says, "The police did a full investigation and found nothing wrong with her." He states that she thinks he is working with the police against her. He says when she is not upset she never accuses him of anything. He says he has tried to talk to her when she is not upset, and she does not seem to remember any of the things she has done. He says that during her last episode he called his sister and asked her to come and watch the children while he took his wife to the hospital. He says she was so upset that she pulled a knife on him and told him she was not going. He says he then took the children and went into the bedroom and locked the door. After a few hours she cried herself to sleep. By morning she was okay and asked him why he and the children were locked in the bedroom.

Mr. Vasquez denies any claims that he has molested his daughter. Mr. Vasquez states that two years ago, when they lived in California, he made a report to the Domestic Violence Court to ensure that he and the children were safe from Mrs. Vasquez. Mr. Vasquez reports that he loves his family. He is willing to do whatever it takes to get this situation under control so that they can "get on with their lives." Mr. Vasquez has made it clear to his wife that they belong together as a family, and that he will not turn his back on her. However, she says "they do not have a family anymore," because she will not tolerate him sexually abusing their child.

The doctor and social worker finally convinced Mrs. Vasquez to let the doctor examine Sarah. Sarah was examined and the medical test did not show any signs of penetration but did show some redness in her vagina and anal area.

Family Background

The Vasquez family lives in a two-bedroom brick house in a very supportive community. They live in a bilingual community where both Spanish and English languages are spoken. The Vasquez family is originally from Mexico, and they speak both Spanish and English. They have been in this community for about a year. Many of their family members live in their neighborhood and are very supportive. The Vasquezes have moved around a lot, searching for work. They are a typical Latino family that is determined to take care of their own family affairs without outsiders' involvement. The Vasquezes have strong work habits. They are both employed and are using their salaries in support of their immediate and extended family members.

Mr. and Mrs. Vasquez have been married for eight years. Mrs. Vasquez was 18 years old and Mr. Vasquez was 30 years old when they were married. The couple migrated from Villa Nueva, Mexico, six months after getting married. Mrs. Vasquez says that the first year of their marriage was the most peaceful.

Melinda Vasquez

Mrs. Vasquez is a medium-built Latino woman. She has black hair and brown eyes. Mrs. Vasquez was born in Villa Nueva, Mexico. She is the seventh of twelve children. All of the siblings live in the United States. Mrs. Vasquez did not graduate from high school; she went as far as the tenth grade. She reports that school in Mexico was not interesting and therefore she chose to work on the family farm. As an adult living in the United States she has a different outlook on education. She hopes to go back to school one day and get her GED. She also says that she expects her children to complete high school and get college degrees. She reports that her family members are farmers by trade. Everyone contributes to ensure that the family needs are met. She states that she has a good relationship with her parents and they keep her "on track" most of the time. Her parents live next door, and her father is retired. Her mother was a housekeeper who works occasionally now sitting with the elderly. Her parents have been in Mexico for the past three months visiting extended family, and they are due to return home in another three months.

Mrs. Vasquez has had several jobs since migrating to the United States. She has been employed as a housekeeper, cook, and a fruit and vegetable packer. She has been working since age 10 and sees employment as a means of providing financial support for the family's basic needs. She is currently employed as a fruit and vegetable packer. She works seven days a week and ten hours a day and is paid less than minimum wage and no overtime.

Mrs. Vasquez reports that their domestic problems began after she became pregnant with their first child. Her husband wanted her to stay at home and she refused. He says that he saw how stressful it was for her to care for the baby and he thought it would be best if she did not work. He says he told her he would work extra hours. He says she refused and became angry and hit him. He says that was the first time she struck him and he did not know what to do, but he assumed that she was just upset or angry. He says that when she got upset he would normally call her mother on the phone, and her mother would be able to calm her down.

Alvin Vasquez, Sr.

Mr. Vasquez is a fairly large man. He is very humble and is known for having a mild personality. He has black hair and light brown eyes. He completed high school and two years of college. Then he went to work in a factory and has since had several factory jobs. He is the third of seven children. He says he has two older sisters who are very nurturing to him. They are like mothers to him, as his mother died when he was 6 years old and his sisters raised him. He has four younger siblings, three brothers and a sister. His three brothers all live in Texas, and his sister and her family lives in California. He says he had a good childhood and he is loved by his family. He states that his sisters have disapproved of the things his wife has put him through and they have asked him to leave and try and take the children. He says he loves his wife and wants his family to be together, but he cannot continue to be accused of a crime like sexual abuse because one day somebody might believe her and he would have to go to jail. He states that he has no criminal record and that he is a good person. He states that everything he has done was to protect his family and provide for them.

Alvin, Jr.

Alvin, Jr., is 5 years old and a very happy little boy. He is very smart and is bilingual. He has a delightful personality and is very strong emotionally. He is enrolled in kindergarten, and he loves school and his teacher. When his abuelo (grandfather) is home, he picks him up from school and he spends the rest of the day with him, his sister Sarah, and four other cousins. He is very close to both parents but does not like to see his father leave home, even to go to work. He has witnessed his mother put his father out of the home on numerous occasions. He gets very scared when his mother is hysterical and he tries to console her when she cries.

Sarah

Sarah is 3 years old and a sickly little girl. Mrs. Vasquez was hospitalized for depression during and after her pregnancy with Sarah. Sarah, however, is very friendly and has a beautiful smile. She has very dark coal-looking hair and beautiful dark brown eyes. She understands Spanish and speaks a few words. She is not very talkative but appears developmentally on target.

SAFETY AND RISK ASSESSMENT QUESTIONS

1. What form of sexual abuse is present in this family?
2. What are the specific injuries and type of abuse to the child or children?
3. What other forms of abuse or neglect are present in this family?
4. How does each of the forms of abuse identified manifest in the family relationships?
5. How do the injuries determine intervention?
6. How does the abuse impact protection of the child or other children in the home?
7. Does the abuse impact family preservation? Explain.

8. What cultural factors must be considered in the determination of what constitutes sexual abuse in this family?

9. How do these factors impact your perception or ability to work with this family?

10. What identifiable situations or patterns contribute to the sexual abuse of the child or children (boundaries, gifts, etc.)?

11. How would your perception change if you were aware of prior abuse to the alleged perpetrator?

FAMILY CASE ANALYSIS—ENGAGEMENT

1. What is the presenting problem? How are the family members involved in the situation defining the problem?

2. In exploring the situation, how does the information that you learn from other family members inform your perceptions?

3. How would you define the working problem based on the current information?

4. What strategies do you think would be useful in engaging with the individuals involved?

FAMILY ASSESSMENT

1. How would your definition of the working problem direct your assessment?

2. What assumptions about human and social behavior are you making, and how would you follow up with these?

3. Are there other problems or issues you think might emerge as you delve deeper into this case? What are they, and how might they affect the situation?

4. What information are you lacking about the situation and its context that you feel you need to know to gain an in-depth understanding?

5. Identify the strengths, limitations, and barriers present in this family. Based on the strengths, where would you start to work with this family?

6. What issues of motivation and/or resistance do you think you are likely to encounter? How do you think you might handle them?

7. Give a clear and concise summary of your assessment, and state how it affects the defining of general goals.

8. Identify and briefly state at least two theoretical frameworks or approaches that would guide your intervention in working with this family.

9. Prepare a genogram and an ecomap for the family, using the blanks given as Figures 5.1 and 5.2.

The _____ Family

☐ Male	▼ Pregnancy	– – – Marital separation
○ Female	×× Death	·–·–· Divorce
		? Whereabouts unknown

FIGURE 5.1   The Family Genogram
(Sketch a genogram of the facts of this family structure.)

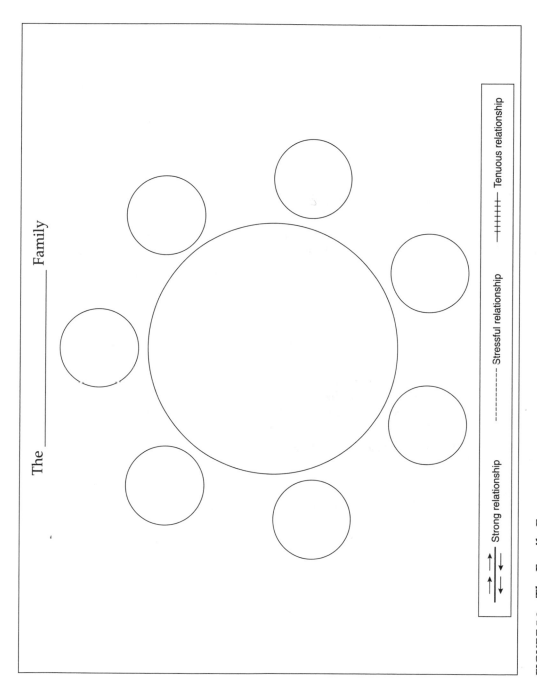

FIGURE 5.2 The Family Ecomap

PLANNING FOR THE FAMILY

1. State your general goals in working with this family.

2. State specific objectives related to each goal, and identify specific changes in the situation that might lead to accomplishing the above goals.

3. What actions should be taken by the worker, the clients, or others to operationalize your objectives?

4. How are you going to set up your evaluation to track accomplishments or progress in goals and objectives? (*Note:* This section should reflect knowledge of methods of practice evaluation.)

FAMILY TREATMENT PLAN/CONTRACT

Design a treatment plan for this family. This is an example of a treatment/contract plan. Most practice texts provide examples.

The Brown Family Treatment/Contract Plan

Client: _____ (Define the client here.)

 I. **Brief Description of the Problem**
(This is generally a summary of the reasons the client came to you or your agency.)

 II. **Primary Goals and Objectives** (Find a format that is clear to your client and you.)

   1. Goal:

       Objective:

   2. Goal:

       Objective:

   3. Goal:

       Objective:

III. We, the undersigned, agree to the following tasks:

　　1.

　　2.

IV. Evaluation of Progress (How your plan will be evaluated.)

_____

_____　　Signature of Social Worker

_____

Signature(s) of Client(s)

_____

(Date)　　　　　　　　　　　　　　　(Date)

SUGGESTED READINGS

Anderson, K. M. (1997). Uncovering survival abilities in children who have been sexually abused. _Families in Society, 78_(6), 592–599.

BajPai, A. (1996). Child sexual abuse: Need for law reforms. _The Indian Journal of Social Work, 57_(4), 630–639.

Bloom, R. B. (1994). Institutional child sexual abuse: Prevention and risk management. _Residential Treatment for Children and Youth, 12_(2), 3–18.

Brown, A., & Finkelhor, D. (1986). Impact of child sexual abuse: A review of the research. _Psychological Bulletin, 99_, 66–77.

Cermark, P., & Molidor, C. (1996). Male victims of child sexual abuse. _Child & Adolescent Social Work Journal, 13_(5), 385–400.

Chandy, J. M., & Blum, R. W. (1996). History of sexual abuse and parental alcohol misuse: Risk, outcomes and protective factors in adolescents. _Child & Adolescent Social Work Journal, 13_(5), 411–432.

Cole, P. M., & Putnam, F. W. (1992). Effect of incest on self and social functioning: A developmental psychopathology perspective. _Journal of Consulting and Clinical Psychology, 60_, 174–184.

Corcoran, J. (1998). In defense of mothers of sexual abuse victims. _Families in Society, 79_(4), 358–369.

DiGiorgio-Miller, J. (1998). Sibling incest: Treatment of the family and the offender. _Child Welfare, 77_(3), 335–346.

Doyle, C. (1996). Sexual abuse by siblings: the victims' perspectives. _The Journal of Sexual Aggression, 2_(1), 17–32.

Humphreys, C. (1995). Counseling and support issues for mothers and fathers of sexually abused children. _Australian Social Work, 48_(4), 13–19.

Jahn, M. F. (1995). Family secrets and family environment: Their relation to later adult functioning. _Alcoholism Treatment Quarterly, 13_(2), 71–80.

Ray, J., Smith, V., & Peterson, T. (1995). A treatment program for children with sexual behavior problems. _Child & Adolescent Social Work Journal, 12_(5), 331–343.

Smith, S. L., Sullivan, Q. E., & Cohen, A. H. (1995). Factors associated with the indication of child abuse reports. _Journal of Social Service Research, 21_(1), 15–34.

CHAPTER SIX

CONTEMPORARY SOCIAL ISSUES

THE MILLER FAMILY (ADOPTION)

Student Instructions

You are employed by the Department of Children and Family Services (DCFS) as an ongoing protective services worker. You have just been assigned the case of a 16-year-old whom the police picked up because his adoptive parents would not allow him to return home. An investigator from your office decided to place the child in custody with the department until someone could work with his parents to try to get him back home. Your job is to make an assessment of the situation and try to return custody to his adoptive parents because there is no place for him in the system. He is currently at an emergency shelter but can stay there for only four more days.

Family Composition

The family consists of the parents, Winston, age 82, and his wife, Geneva, age 70. They have two adopted sons, Melvin, age 16, and Delbert, age 15. Melvin's biological mother, Stacey Livingston, age 31, and her son, Isadore, age 12, are involved with the family. Mrs. Miller also has two biological sons from her previous marriage who are involved with this family. They are Vincent, age 50, and Abraham, age 48.

Current Situation

The Department of Children and Family Services (DCFS) was contacted after Melvin Miller was not allowed to return to the home of his adoptive parents. Melvin left the home of his adoptive parents approximately seven months ago and was living in the home of his biological mother. Melvin was told to leave his mother's home because of his negative behavior and his refusal to go to school. Melvin returned to his adoptive parents' home, but he was informed that he could not live in their home any longer. The adoptive parents have been upset over this whole ordeal and they are considering whether to allow Melvin to return home. The adoptive father is 82 years old and the mother is 70. They have not totally given up on Melvin, but they do not want him to live in their home at this time. Information received from the case file and the prior case worker indicated that Melvin has been living with his adoptive parents off and on since he was 3 years old. However, he was not adopted by them until right before his sixth birthday. When Melvin turned 4, he went back to live with his biological mother, Stacey Livingston, for six months. She became involved with drugs and he was placed back into the Millers's home. When Melvin turned 5, his mother's parental rights were terminated. However, she continued to play a role in his life. The Millers state that they understand the developmental, emotional, physical, and educational needs of children like Melvin. The family consistently met his needs until Melvin voluntarily left the home to live with his biological mother. Ms. Livingston works at the Waffle House, which is within walking distance of her small two-bedroom apartment. She has one son, Isadore, 12, who lives with her. He was also placed in foster care when he was about a year old, but she managed to get herself together and she was given back custody of him when he was 4.

The Millers are aware that they are under investigation based on the fact that they did not let Melvin back into the home. They are willing to work with DCFS to ensure he receives counseling services. The Millers are very upset that Melvin does not seem to respect them or the rules of their home. Melvin is one of two boys whom the Millers adopted. They expect Melvin to be an example to his younger brother who lives in their home.

Family Background

Winston was born in Jackson, Mississippi, and Geneva Miller was born in Sparta, Mississippi. They met in California and were married in 1954. This African American family moved from San Francisco, California to Columbus, Georgia. The couple adopted two boys, Melvin and Delbert. The family is upper middle class. Mrs. Miller has two biological sons from a former marriage. Both of her sons live in Mississippi. They have three children each, and the Millers are very involved with their grandchildren. They believe in hard work; education is seen as preparation for living a responsible and productive life. Mr. and Mrs. Miller attended a community college and had hoped to live long enough to see Melvin and Delbert graduate from college.

They have prepared financially to send them to college. Mrs. Miller's sons are both educated, and she is very proud of how they became two very responsible men in society. Both adopted boys are expected to obey the law, attend school, respect others' property, and participate in church activities. When the boys were smaller, their parents used corporal punishment, time outs, removal of privileges, and restrictions as means of discipline. Mrs. Miller administers the punishments, and Mr. Miller considers himself the peacemaker in the home.

Winston and Geneva Miller

Winston Miller is an 82-year-old man who is healthy and actively employed. He has gray hair and dark brown eyes. Geneva Miller is a 70-year-old woman who is recovering from a stroke she suffered during surgery on her left knee. She also reports having high blood pressure and is on medication. She has black and gray hair and beautiful brown eyes. Both Mr. and Mrs. Miller are very pleasant people to talk to. Both are retired from their professions. Mrs. Miller managed a day care for forty years, and Mr. Miller worked in a funeral home, where he is currently employed part-time. They were foster parents for DCFS until about five years ago, when they stopped in order to dedicate more of their time to the boys.

Melvin Miller

Melvin is 5 feet 9 inches tall, with black hair and brown eyes, and wears glasses. He has a missing tooth in the upper front of his mouth, which he has not wanted to get fixed because he thinks it is rather "sexy." Melvin attended counseling about four years ago as a result of aggressive behavior. The Millers think he might be using marijuana. He has admitted being involved with a gang and has stated that they do commit crimes, but that he has not participated in any crime so far.

Melvin is an intelligent teenager with great academic potential. Up until about two years ago he was a straight A student. He has stated in the past that he loves school. His emotions seems to vacillate from high to low with little provocation. He is not afraid to initiate fights with peers of the opposite sex. He is very disrespectful to females, including his adoptive mother. He recently admitted to being sexually active and has stated to his adoptive mother that he hopes to get his girlfriend pregnant so that he can have his own child. He stated that he would never put his child up for adoption. He appears very self-centered and has stated that he does not care about anybody except himself. He appears to be obsessed with having money. He has even stated that he would do anything to have money, even if it meant stealing or robbing someone. He is very interested in knowing why his mother gave him up for adoption. He states that he loves his adoptive parents, and he feels abandoned by them at this time. He has a special relationship with his adoptive father, but he and his adoptive mother have had problems in their relationship for a few years.

According to his adoptive brother, Melvin is the favorite child in the home. He gets a lot of privileges and chances. His brother also states that Melvin tries to push him around. He has started fights with his brother, and on one occasion he broke his brother's leg. He said it was an accident. He has been involved in many physical fights at school, and each time someone is hurt. Additionally, he has threatened adult authority figures at school and at church. Melvin is aware that his privileges and chances have come to an end and now he has to pay the consequences of his behavior. However, he wants to do it his way and expects everyone to forgive him and give him another chance. Mrs. Miller is somewhat afraid of Melvin now and is not comfortable letting him back in the house. Mr. Miller would like to see him return home but is afraid for Mrs. Miller and their other son.

Delbert

Delbert is 15 and a very shy and friendly young man. He is not Melvin's biological brother. He has tried not to get involved with what Melvin is doing. He was adopted at birth by the Millers and does not know his biological parents. He has stated that he has no interest in finding them at this time. Delbert is in junior ROTC at his high school and hopes to enter the military after college. He loves Melvin but states that Melvin does not like him. He has tried to keep Melvin's secrets, but whenever he thinks they might hurt someone he feels responsible. He is very close to his mother and hates the way that Melvin treats her. Delbert is very close to Geneva's biological sons and often visits them in the summer. He and Melvin used to travel together, but Melvin does not like to visit them anymore. Delbert states that he is not sexually active but is very interested in girls.

THE GOMEZ FAMILY (IMMIGRATION)

Student Instructions

You are a protective services investigator with the Department of Children and Family Services (DCFS). You have just been assigned to investigate allegations of possible educational and medical neglect.

Family Composition

The Gomez family is from Panama. They reside in a rural area in the Midwest region of the United States. The family consists of the father, Antonio, age 35, the mother, Isolina, age 30, and their two children, Maria, age 10, and Gustovo, who is 6 years old.

Current Situation

The Gomez family came to the attention of DCFS after an anonymous call was received. The caller stated that Maria and Gustovo do not attend school and are staying with a babysitter all day, together with several other unidentified children. Recently, Gustovo has been ill with flu symptoms, and now his illness has progressed. He appears to have lesions all over his body, a very high temperature, and is losing weight. According to the reporter, the babysitter has on several occasions been unable to wake Gustovo up after a nap. The babysitter has talked to the parents and they have been using home remedies, but the child's illness continues to progress. According to the reporter, the mother and father are reluctant to take the child to a hospital.

After the report was made, DCFS went to the babysitter's home to assess the situation. Gustovo was found in a fetal position with what appeared to be a high temperature and lesions all over his face, and he appeared to be unconscious. The babysitter stated that she had been giving him cough medicine and children's Tylenol for three weeks. She also stated that she has been trying to wake him up for the last thirty minutes. The investigator immediately called an ambulance and Gustovo was transported to the emergency room at the hospital in town. Once doctors were able to stabilize him, Gustovo was airlifted to a pediatric treatment center. After four hours of triage and treatment, Gustovo was diagnosed with a severe case of tuberculosis. The doctors are asking for his parents and the names of anyone who has been in contact with Gustovo in the last month.

The parents went to the babysitter's home to pick up Maria and Gustovo and learned that Gustovo had been taken to the hospital. The DCFS investigator was at the babysitter's home and advised the parents of Gustovo's condition. The parents were very upset, and both cried and wanted to see Gustovo right away. The investigator advised them that they needed to go to the hospital and take Maria, along with the children's medical records.

Family Background

The Gomez family reports that they migrated to the Midwest after a short stop in California to obtain funds and necessary clothing. They were transported to the United States under an illegal work contract that guaranteed work, housing, and eventual permanency. To date, the family has no legal documentation allowing them to remain in the United States. The family are native Panamanians. They traveled from Panama City, Panama, to Mexico City, Mexico, and finally arrived in the United States six months ago. The family's extended family are residents of Panama City. The family support system in the United States consists of two Panamanian families and three families from Mexico City, Mexico. The six families traveled to the United States under the same conditions.

Antonio Gomez

Antonio is the fifth son in a family of ten children. He observed how his family struggled through the transitions of the Panamanian economy. His family's main income was a result of the agricultural efforts of his parents, Alberto and Eneida Gomez. Antonio was the first of his siblings to finish high school. He was determined not to be a farmer. He had plans to attend the University of Panama School of Business. However, after his fiancé Isolina became pregnant, he decided to go to work to support her and the baby. After the baby was born they talked about moving to the United States for a better life for themselves and their child. He also wanted to prove to his parents that he could care for his family without farming.

Antonio obtained minimum-wage jobs and supported his family in the best way he could. Of course, he was aware that his education limited his income, and though he searched for ways to improve his family's life, he found himself working all the time just to make ends meet. He was frustrated and discouraged, so he made contact with some family friends who were Panamanian immigrants living in the United States. Their success in the United States increased his motivation to leave Panama. He and his wife filed for visas to leave Panama to visit the United States. He received a letter from the U.S. Consulate in Panama City saying that his visa request would be delayed because of a waiting list that was ten to twelve years long. He and his wife decided to seek other alternatives that would get them to the United States sooner. They made it to the United States.

Isolina Gomez

Isolina was known as the "most likely to succeed" among her high school peers. She was the first of three children born to the Contreras. The Contreras are a progressive Panamanian family. They were among the first generation of professional Panamanian families, and among the initial participants in Panamanian industrial development. Isolina's father, Santiago Contreras, is an electrical engineer, and her mother, Sabina Contreras, is a special education teacher. Isolina's parents had high expectations for her, and she was called "the physician." Before becoming pregnant she wanted to go to medical school to become a doctor. She was a helper and always read medical books, and she would patch up the dogs in the community and diagnose her parents and grandparents whenever one had an illness. Her parents were really disappointed when she became pregnant before marriage and before going to college. Isolina felt that she had not only let her parents down but that she had let herself down. But she loved her husband and they decided that they would make a better life for themselves. When they got to the United States, Isolina would go to medical school.

THE KELLEY FAMILY (TERMINATION OF PARENTAL RIGHTS)

Student Instructions

You are a social worker with the Department of Children and Family Services (DCFS) pre-adoption unit. Your agency has been working with this family for five years. The children have previously been in foster care. The case is being transferred to your unit for evaluation for possible foster care placement or termination of parental rights.

Family Composition

The Kelley family consists of the mother, Cecilia, age 23, and her three children. She has two sons, Marvin, age 5, and Rodney, age 2. She has one daughter, Lavern, age 8 months. Ms. Kelley's uncle, Hank Pitman, lives in the home and has served as a caretaker for the children.

Current Situation

Cecilia Kelley, a 23-year-old mother, was arrested for attempting to buy crack cocaine. When the police took her to the police station she told them that she could not be locked up because she had three small children at home. She also told the police that if her social worker found out, "they might take her children." She told them that her children were alone in the house. The police took Ms. Kelley to her house, and when they arrived, her uncle Hank was there. Hank told her that he would watch the children until she got out of jail. Ms. Kelley's boyfriend, Roger Davis , bailed her out of jail. The police made a report to DCFS. Ms. Kelley was told by her social worker that if she received another report of using or attempting to buy cocaine, the children might be removed from the home.

Family Background

Ms. Kelley has been known to the department for five years. Her son, Marvin, was born addicted to cocaine. She has attempted on several occasions to stay clean. She has been in six drug treatment programs. Four years ago Cecilia had a baby that she gave up for adoption. The baby was a little girl and was born with health problems due to Cecilia's drug use. The adoption was handled by Children's Society Adoption Agency. Cecilia did not want to give her baby up for adoption but felt that she could not care for her. Three years ago, Marvin was placed in foster care for six months. Two years ago, Rodney was born a cocaine-addicted baby. At that time, both Marvin and Rodney were placed in foster care because a case worker went to the home and found Ms. Kelley high on drugs; there was no food or milk for the baby, and the home was not "fit for human habitation." The boys stayed in a foster home for four months while Ms. Kelley completed drug treatment and found another place to live. Lavern is Ms. Kelley's first child born not addicted to cocaine. However, one month after Lavern was born Ms. Kelley tested positive for marijuana and cocaine. She went into an outpatient treatment program but did not complete the program.

Cecilia Kelley

Cecilia Kelley was born in an urban area in the Midwest and is the second youngest of five children. Cecilia has lost 83 pounds in the last six months. Her hair has fallen out and she is very weak. Cecilia has always been a well-built woman. Her parents are Betty Kelley and Frank Smith. Cecilia's mother has been separated from Mr. Smith for twenty years, but they never divorced. Both of her parents live nearby and have regular contact with Cecilia and her children. Cecilia stated that her family never lived in one place for more than six months. She says they moved from one city to another. She says she and her siblings had a hard time staying in school because they moved so frequently. Cecilia did not finish high school but hopes to go back and finish one day.

Cecilia states that most or all of her relationships have been unstable. Her parents have never been a strong support to her, although they have always been in her life. She also says that all of the men she has had in her life have been either abusive or alcoholics, until two years ago when she met Roger Davis. She says Roger is a 27-year-old Caucasian man who has been very good to her and the children. Cecilia thinks that Roger is the father of her youngest child. However, Roger states that he is not the father of any of Cecilia's children. He does, however, pay child support to Cecilia for Lavern. According to Cecilia, Roger spends a lot of time with her and the children. He spends the night occasionally and if she needs anything for any of the children, he provides it. According to Roger, Cecilia is not his girlfriend. He says that he met her at a club and every now and then they see each other and he gives her some money. Cecilia says that a year ago he found out that she was using drugs and told her that he would not have anything further to do with her. She says, however, that "he always answers my page"; therefore she considers him her boyfriend. Cecilia says in the last six months she has not been able to get in touch with him. She says he mails her some money every month for the children. She says he has asked her to stop calling him. Cecilia states that six months ago she told him that she was going to kill herself if he did not come over and talk to her. She said he came over and they had sex and now she is five months pregnant and she believes that he is the father. She is afraid to tell him for fear that he will leave her and she will never hear from him again. She says that her children love him and she does not know what she will do without the extra money. She also says that he is the first man who has not been abusive to her. Cecilia also noted that her two oldest children, Marvin and Rodney, have different fathers and that she has not heard from the fathers or seen them since she was pregnant. She says she is not even sure who their fathers are. She admits getting pregnant when she was on a drug binge and had sex with several people.

Cecilia states that she has a close relationship with her mother, Betty Kelley, and her uncle, Hank Pitman. Mr. Pitman resides with the family on a temporary basis and is the secondary caretaker of the children. Cecilia's mother, Betty Kelley, also has regular contact with Cecilia. She resides in a one-bedroom apartment, several units down from Cecilia's apartment. Cecilia states that she has frequent contact with her father, Frank Smith, and that her father provides guidance and support whenever he can. Cecilia states that her father and mother have had substance abuse problems for many years. She says they are heroin users. Her father is employed as a taxi driver and provides transportation for Cecilia to do her shopping and other errands. Cecilia states that her father is aware of her substance abuse problem, and has told her that she should not use drugs. She says that her father will not get high with her. He has told her that "he better not see her get high." However, she has gotten high with her mother many times.

According to Cecilia's social worker, she generally keeps appointments when she is not using drugs. If she has to cancel an appointment she will notify the social worker that she needs to reschedule. Cecilia continues to maintain marginally adequate supervision, clothing, and food supply for her children when the rent and utilities have been paid for the month. In addition, her social worker says that whenever Cecilia has someone living with her she can pay her rent and utilities. However, usually after two or three months the person moves out because Cecilia does not pay her part of the rent and usually has used her money for drugs.

Whenever Cecilia is not using drugs, her interaction with her children is very good. She laughs and plays with them and oversees Marvin's homework. Marvin is attending elementary school and is receiving satisfactory grades. During home visits, the social worker had noted that Cecilia interacts in a positive and affectionate manner toward her children, and responds quickly to their needs. Cecilia's children have difficulties with delayed gratification; Rodney and Lavern frequently whine and cry. Although Cecilia has expressed frustration with handling her children's misbehavior, Cecila usually responds to these behaviors in a nonthreatening manner. The social worker noted that she observed a situation where Cecilia utilized corporal punishment (spanking) on Marvin and Rodney for their whining and arguing. Rodney and Lavern have not had their shots, and they are in need of physical examinations.

Cecilia resides in a one-bedroom apartment along with her uncle, and her children. Cecilia has converted the living room into a second bedroom, and has recently obtained a queen-size bed and a twin-size bed for the family. Cecilia and 8-month old Lavern occupy the queen-size bed, while Marvin and Rodney share the twin-size bed. Hank Pitman uses the existing bedroom.

Marvin

Marvin is 5 years old and very friendly. Marvin is smart and loves school. He is very protective of his mother. Marvin says he wishes he had a father. He says that every "daddy" he gets leaves him. Marvin is liked by his teacher, and she spends a lot of time with him. Cecilia has allowed Marvin to spend the night with his teacher. Marvin's past foster parents always inquire about him and wonder how he is doing. Marvin told Cecilia that he wishes they could all go and live with his foster parents, Mr. and Mrs. Raine. They were very good to Marvin and wanted to adopt him. However, he was returned home for the second time. Marvin is very close to Rodney. He is like a caretaker for Rodney. He has been left home on numerous occasions to care for himself and Rodney.

Rodney

Rodney, age 2, is a shy little boy. He is small for his age, but the doctors say he is developmentally on target. Rodney was a cocaine baby. He is not bonded to Cecilia; he is bonded to Marvin. Marvin is able to calm him down when he is tired or sick. Rodney will allow Cecilia to hold him but does not look to Cecilia for comfort. He has been in foster care and was well cared for by his foster parents, Mr. and Mrs. Brown. The Browns wish they could adopt Rodney. When Rodney was first in their home he was malnourished and would not speak. After two months he had gained weight and was learning to talk. He cried when he had to leave the Brown home. However, the social worker took Marvin with her to pick up Rodney, and that made it easier for Rodney to leave the Browns.

Lavern

Lavern is 8 months old and is developmentally delayed. She is very small and is frequently sick. She cries a lot and is very irritable. Lavern smiles on occasion and is a lovable baby. She loves to be held and is somewhat bonded to Cecilia.

THE WELLINGTON-SAMPSON FAMILY
(ADOLESCENT WITH INDEPENDENT
LIVING ISSUES)

Student Instructions

You are an outreach worker with a local child welfare agency and you are working with the transitional program. Your agency has just received a call from Verna Sampson requesting some kind of help for her husband's younger brother Cyril Wellington, who is presently living with their family.

Family Composition

The Wellington-Sampson family consists of Cyril Wellington, who is 17 years old, his brother, Carl Sampson, and Mr. Sampson's wife, Verna, both in their 30s, and the Sampsons' two children, Sylvia, age 9, and Matthew, age 7.

Current Situation

Cyril Wellington is 17 years old. He has been involved with one social service agency or another almost all his life. He was the youngest son of Sally Wellington, who was almost 45 years old when Cyril was born. By the time of his birth, his brother Carl was 13 years old and had been living with his paternal grandparents for seven years. Carl and the grandparents were estranged from his mother and were unaware of Cyril's birth because they were living in another state. Cyril has had several major transitions in his life and is now undergoing another one; he has moved in with his brother, Mr. Sampson. Previously, Cyril was not even aware that he had a brother.

Family Background

At the age of 5, Cyril was removed from his mother's custody for neglect and placed in the foster home of Mrs. Jasper. Mrs. Jasper became ill and Cyril was removed from her care. This placement had been very successful, and Cyril was devastated in having to leave Mrs. Jasper's home. He called Mrs. Jasper "Mom." He was placed in another home at the age of 13. However, the second placement did not work out. Cyril began to fall behind in school and became belligerent with his foster parents. He ran away on two occasions; on both occasions he was trying to get to Mrs. Jasper's house, which was about fifty miles away, but he was caught and put in detention for being a runaway. While in detention he was evaluated and was assessed as being depressed, possibly having paranoid thoughts, and displaying violent behaviors with staff. He was placed in a treatment institution for adolescents. After an initial period of difficulty, he seemed to adjust to the routine and most of his symptoms subsided. During this time, he says he tried to write to Mrs. Jasper, but the letters were returned as undeliverable. He has tried calling her, but her number has been disconnected. He called her neighbor's house and was told that she is in a nursing home but they did not know which one.

Cyril was then moved into an institution where he finished high school. Records at the institution described him as quiet and a loner, but with no documented behavior problems. At this point it was deemed that a search for relatives was necessary because he was nearing the age of 18. Cyril's social worker was able to locate his brother Carl. When Carl received the call stating that he had a brother, he was very shocked because he was not aware that he had a sibling. He agreed to allow Cyril to stay with them until a more permanent arrangement could be worked out.

Mrs. Sampson fixed up a finished area in their basement for Cyril to stay in. They made him a bedroom and a small sitting room. Cyril has been with them for six months. Mrs. Sampson and her husband both say that Cyril appears to be a nice young man and they have not had any serious problems with him. They state that Cyril spends most of his time in his room watching television. Mr. Sampson says he frequently leaves the house late at night and is gone for several hours and no one knows where he is. According to Cyril, he is just out playing pool or walking around the lake near the house. He says sometimes he just walks around the neighborhood and watches people. Mrs. Sampson thinks this behavior is "sort of creepy." She says that she and her husband have tried to talk to Cyril about plans for his future, but he acts anxious, nervous, and withdrawn and then goes to his room. Mr. Sampson states that when they approach him with the idea of going through the process of emancipation and becoming independent, he just clams up and shuts down. It usually takes him about a week to warm back up to them. Lately he will not take his meals with them, and if he is pushed to eat with them he will not eat anything. Mr. Sampson says he will do everything he can for Cyril, but that Cyril cannot live in their basement forever.

Cyril has expressed a desire to move out of his brother's home one day and get a job. He has also thought of going into the Air Force, but when asked if he has made any plans to try and make these things happen, he says nothing. He has been asked what kind of job he would like and he says he does not know but maybe he could work in a restaurant. However, he also states that he does not like talking to people. Cyril said to his brother, "People make me nervous."

THE CHRISTIE FAMILY (PERMANENCY)

Student Instructions

You are a foster care worker with the Department of Children and Family Services (DCFS). You have been working with the Christie family for over two years. You have had to place the children in foster care because of parental neglect and continued substance abuse. You will need to assess the case for permanency or continued foster care. The children have been in foster care for three years.

Family Composition

The Christie family consists of the father, Joel, age 68, the mother, Alicia, age 40, and their seven children. They have four sons, Bert, age 16, Dennis, age 11, Dave, age 9, and Steve, age 7. They have twin girls, Thelma and Velma, who are 5 years old. The Christie's also have an older daughter, Barbara, age 23, who is not in the home. She is married and has two children, Enrique, age 3, and Orville, age 2. Barbara and her family reside out of state and visit about once a year. Mr. Stan Simpson is not in the home but is a significant adult in the children's lives. He is believed to have fathered Mrs. Christie's four younger children. Mrs. Christie had an affair with him while she was separated from Mr. Christie. The children call him Uncle Stan.

Current Situation

The Christie children are currently in three different foster homes. They were placed in foster care due to their mother's continued substance abuse and neglect of them. Mrs. Christie's four younger children all tested positive for cocaine and marijuana at birth. The children were initially placed with Mr. Christie while Mrs. Christie was in drug treatment. However, she left treatment after one week and refused to complete the program. After she returned home she started using again on a regular basis, and as a result the children were again placed in foster care temporarily. Mrs. Christie was devastated and agreed to return to treatment, and Mr. Christie agreed to go to a support group. Two months later the children were returned to the physical custody of the father, but legal custody remained with DCFS. Three months later, Mr. Christie moved out of the house after a domestic dispute in which Mrs. Christie jumped on him because he would not give her any money or take her to buy drugs. When Mr. Christie moved out, Mrs. Christie would not allow him to take the children. Two days later she asked him to move back home, but he refused. Mrs. Christie was very angry, so she took an overdose of pills and was rushed to the hospital. Bert, her oldest son, had found her lying on the floor in the bedroom, and he called the police. Mr. Christie was out of town with his mother, and the children were picked up again and returned to foster care. Fortunately for the children, they were all placed back into their previous foster homes. Because they are in three different homes, it is difficult for them to see each other on a regular basis, and they are having a hard time adjusting to foster care.

Family Background

Prior to placement, the family lived in a large, five-bedroom frame home. The home was adequate to meet the basic needs of the family. The community from which this family comes can be viewed as both stressful and supportive. Extended family live in the area. Mrs. Christie says that although they have family and friends, there is no one she can consistently count on for help when she needs it. Other governmental agencies are involved with this family. The family receives financial support from several government programs. Mr. Christie receives Social Security and a retirement pension from the U.S. Postal Service. The family also receives food stamps.

The parents state that they are willing to get back together if they can be reunited with their children right away. Mrs. Christie says she wants her children back and would do anything to have them returned. However, the parents' actions have demonstrated limited motivation to resolve the issues that initially brought the family to the attention of the department. The children have been in the custody of the department for the last three years. Mrs. Christie was informed of the fact that her relapse and refusal to obtain and maintain sobriety has jeopardized her chances of the children being returned right away. Mrs. Christie continues to use drugs. She stated that she did not think DCFS would take her children from her. Mr. Christie does not drink or use drugs, but he supports his wife in her behaviors. Most of the children want to go home to their parents. The oldest child, Bert, is aware of everything, and he has told his mother and father that if his mother does not stop using, they might never be able to come back home.

Joel Christie

Mr. Christie is African American. He was born in Houston, Texas. He is an only child, and he was raised in a single-parent home. He is very close to his mother and visits her on a daily basis. His mother was 14 years old when he was born. He did not develop a relationship with his father until after he was an adult. When he was 40 years old his parents married. His father died ten years ago, but he is very happy that he had an opportunity to build a relationship with him even though it was short. He states that his mother made sure he had a wonderful childhood. He does not remember any violent episodes because his mother did not allow men to stay with them. He states that his mother was a very hardworking woman and she instilled in him a strong work ethic. Mr. Christie went to college and received a B.S. in engineering. He retired five years ago from the Postal Service after thirty-seven years of service. Mr. Christie states that he has a heart condition. Right before he retired he suffered a massive heart attack and had to have open-heart surgery.

Mr. Christie states that this is his second marriage. He first got married when he was 26 years old, and he and his wife were married for twenty years. He has two children from that marriage who live in Arizona. His son is a doctor and his daughter is a lawyer. He is not in contact with them much, but goes to visit them occasionally. Two years after his divorce he married Alicia and they have seven children. They have had a lot of problems but he feels she needs someone to look after her and the children and that is why he has tried to maintain the relationship. He says his emotional support comes from his mother and he could not make it without her. He says his mother is disappointed in him.

Alicia Christie

Mrs. Christie is Caucasian. She was born in Jackson, Mississippi. She is the fourth of six children. Both of her parents are deceased. She states that her childhood was somewhat volatile and that she and her siblings were physically abused as children. She remembers that on one occasion they were taken from her parents for one week after both of her parents were arrested for public drunkenness. She also states that she and her two younger siblings were removed from her mother's custody when she was 9 years old, after her mother went to prison for killing their father. She states that her three older siblings were sent to live with a relative in another state. Ten years ago, her mother died in prison from cancer. Mrs. Christie attended high school and completed the eleventh grade. She states that she would like to work but she does not seem to be able to hold a job. She is reportedly in fair health but has had two gall stone surgeries. She reports using drugs for approximately ten years. She has been in drug and alcohol treatment on four occasions.

Mrs. Christie states that this is her first marriage and that her husband has been very good to her. She says she has not been a good wife to him but she thinks she loves him. She says her husband is a "Mr. Good Guy." When she met him she was not using drugs, though on occasion she would have a beer. She reports having had a lot of problems with the law and that her husband always rescues her. She has been arrested for driving without a license, driving while intoxicated, fighting, and also for stealing her husband's car, trading it for drugs, and then reporting it stolen.

Mrs. Christie states that her life has been "hell." She reports having no friends and says she trusts no one. However, she does depend on her husband for financial and emotional support, and she depends on Mr. Simpson to help her with the children. She states that Mr. Simpson thinks that he might be the father of her four younger children, but he keeps quiet and just helps her out with child care and things the children need. She says the children love him and spend about two weekends out of the month with him. Mr. Christie allows Mr. Simpson to spend the weekends with them because Mr. Simpson is not allowed to take the children to his own house; the woman he is living with will not allow it.

Bert

Bert is 16 years old and in high school. He is very quiet and has been in a paternal role most of his life. He is a good student but has missed a lot of school to care for his siblings. He is not adjusting well to foster care. However, the foster parents state that he is very polite and they have no problems with him. It is clear to them that Bert has chosen not to bond with them. On three occasions Bert was late coming home from school and Dennis told the foster mother that Bert had to go home and see about their mom. His case worker has told him that they cannot go home right now.

Dennis

Dennis is 11 years old. Dennis is quiet and passive, but an angry young boy. He is in fourth grade, and he does not like school. He has failed two grades. This is his first year in special education and he is withdrawn. He is, however, doing much better because his foster parents are dedicating a lot of time to helping him. He is very attached to Bert and depends on him for emotional support. Dennis is enjoying his foster home, but he knows that Bert does not like it there, so he pretends not to like it either. Whenever Bert is not home, Dennis tells his foster mother how much he loves her cooking and he asks her questions such as "If we have to leave home again, can we come here?" The foster mother says that Dennis has asked her if she could keep all of them so that they could be together.

Dave

Dave is 9 years old, friendly, and very independent. He has an outgoing personality and enjoys being the life of the party. He has a good sense of humor and knows how to make everyone laugh. Dave is also in fourth grade and is very smart. He is not attached to his mother, but he is very attached to his father. He does not mention his mother at all. He has told his foster parents that if his father would leave his mother, they could go home. Dennis is very angry at his mother and does not want to go home as long as she is there. Whenever they have a visit with their mother he goes into the bathroom and will not come out until the visit is over. His father has only visited with them on three occasions; Mr. Christie has been sick and is now living with his mother.

Steve

Steve is 7 years old and a very happy child. His personality is a lot like Dave's, but he does not show his anger. Steve is in first grade and he loves school. Steve is attached to their foster parents. He calls them "Mom" and "Dad." He has told Dave that he never wants to go home.

Thelma and Velma

Thelma and Velma are 5-year-old twins. They are in the same foster home, and they are very attached to their foster parents. Their foster parents are a young professional couple who could not have children. Each of the girls has her own room. They are in kindergarten and are very good students. They are Brownie Scouts, and they sing in the children's choir at church.

They miss their siblings and ask to visit them, but they do not like to visit their parents. They call their foster parents "Mom" and "Dad." They are very happy girls and have asked their foster parents if they can live with them forever.

THE BENNINGAN-RIVERS FAMILY (LESBIAN COUPLE ADOPTION)

Student Instruction

You are a social worker with the Department of Children and Family Services (DCFS) Adoption Unit. You are doing a home study on a lesbian couple who would like to adopt another child. They have specifically requested to adopt a male child of any race. They already have an adopted daughter who is biracial. Other community factors and community concerns are also affecting this case.

Family Composition

The Benningan-Rivers family consists of the mother, Della Bennigan, age 36, and her partner, Lee Rivers, age 33. They have one adopted daughter, Leslie, age 5. Ms. Benningan adopted Leslie when she was 1 year old. Ms. Rivers has been in the home since Leslie was adopted. Ms. Benningan and Ms. Rivers have been together for eight years. Although their intention to adopt is mutual, Della will be the "Mom," with Lee taking on the role of "Aunt." Both will provide care and will share decision-making responsibilities. Leslie has adapted well, and she calls Ms. Benningan "Mom" and Ms. Rivers "Auntie."

Current Situation

This lesbian couple is in the process of adopting a second child. Your agency received a call from a local concerned citizens group, stating that they have heard from a neighbor of the lesbian couple that they were in the process of adopting a child. The information was shared with several people, and they do not think it is in the best interest of a child to be in a home with homosexuals. The concerned citizens want to share their concerns about the ramifications of the well-being of this child with your agency. They are threatening a lawsuit against your agency if the adoption is approved. They also state that they plan to go to the media with their concerns, and that they will protest in front of your office.

Family Background

Ms. Benningan and Ms. Rivers have been partners for approximately eight years. They consider themselves married. They have had a lot of difficulty with people not respecting their choice to share their lives with each other, and they are very supportive of each other. Ms. Benningan states she has always wanted to be a mother, and after she entered a relationship with Lee they decided to become foster parents. She states they were both certified as foster parents, but no children were ever placed with them. She stated that they decided to adopt and realized that they would run into problems if they tried to adopt together. She states that she completed the adoption process and three months later adopted their daughter Leslie, when Leslie was a year old. When Leslie turned 5, they decided that they wanted to adopt a son. They were watching television and saw a little boy on television who was available for adoption. The little boy is deaf, and they think they can help him because both of them know sign language.

Della and Lee have a circle of friends, and they also rely heavily on their families for support. Della relies on her best friend Olivia at work, because she and her husband have adopted four children. Della states that Olivia has been an asset and a resource for them because she often allows Leslie to spend the night and play with her children.

Della and Lee indicate that they each have a healthy attitude regarding sex. When asked to address normal developmental stages, including sexuality, Della indicated that since she has no experience discussing the topic of human sexuality with a child, she would need to look for additional training and obtain books from the library for assistance. She also states that their son would have adult males in his life who would fill a mentoring role. If other problems occurred, they both state that the companies they work for have individual and family counseling services available. They admit that there may be problems, but they will do everything in their power to ensure that the child has a healthy upbringing. They do not want to be judged for their choice to share their lives.

Della stated that they are aware that there are considerations in placing a child in a two-female, openly lesbian household. She stated that they would like to have several preplacement visits, to allow the child to feel comfortable in their home and get to know them. When asked how she would help a child make the transition to their home, she replied that they would involve the child with some of their male friends and other families they know who have adopted. They stated that their son would be reared in a loving extended family that is culturally diverse and very accepting of differences. They stated that Leslie has adjusted well.

Della Benningan

Ms. Benningan is a 36-year-old biracial woman who is the second oldest of five children. Her parents divorced when she was 6 years old. Her father was granted full custody of all of them. He remarried when she was 8 and she had a very close relationship with her stepmother. Her stepmother later legally adopted all of them. Della's parents live nearby and are very supportive of their children. Ms. Benningan states that about every two or three years she hears from her biological mother, but they do not have a close relationship.

Ms. Benningan states that she had a "normal" childhood. She was allowed to participate in extracurricular activities at school. Her family was very involved in community and church activities. She ran track in high school and received the citizenship award when she was a senior. She considers herself fortunate because her stepmother was her "mother" and friend. She describes her stepmother as being loving, gentle, a good listener, and warm. She describes her father as loving, consistent, and understanding. She states that most of the people in her life were very loving and accepting of her. She does not remember having many fights with them when she was a teenager.

Ms. Benningan has been in same-sex relationships for fifteen years. She stated that she had her first relationship with a woman while she was in college. That relationship lasted for three years, and it was devastating when her lover terminated the relationship to marry a man and have children. She states she did not date seriously for about two years after that. She states that her stepmother helped her through the ordeal. She is grateful for the experience, because she learned about commitment versus desire and all of the pressures that go with choosing to have a relationship with someone of the same sex. She stated that while in high school she dated males but always had close female relationships. She finished college with a B.S. degree in business management.

Lee Rivers

Ms. Rivers is a 33-year-old Caucasian woman who is the middle child of ten children. Her parents divorced when she was 16 years old. Both of her parents remarried. Her mother and stepfather live nearby. She does not communicate with them at all. Her father lives on the West Coast, and they are in contact with each other on a weekly basis. Her father is very supportive of her, although he does not agree with her all of her choices. Her brother and sisters all live nearby, with the exception of two sisters who live on the East Coast. She and Ms. Benningan, along with their daughter, visit her father every New Year's.

Ms. Rivers graduated from high school but never went to college. After high school, she got a job working at a large industrial plant making refrigerators. She has been at that job for eighteen years. Lee says that she has a few health problems. She says she suffers from asthma, and also that she has a history of mild depression for which she takes Prozac.

THE COOPER FAMILY
(JUVENILE DELINQUENCY)

Student Instructions

You are a social worker with the Children's Community Youth Diversion Agency. You will be working with Larry Cooper, Jr., and his family. You must make an assessment of Larry's situation and his family. You will need to report your assessment to the Juvenile Court.

Family Composition

The household consists of the parents, Larry Cooper, Sr., age 44, his wife, Nina Cooper, age 40, and their children, Jennifer, age 15, Larry, Jr., age 12, and LaDonna, age 2. Mrs. Cooper's mother, Mrs. Fannie Hayes, age 62, also lives with the family.

Current Situation

Larry Cooper, Jr., was brought to the Community Youth Diversion Agency by his parents, Larry Cooper, Sr., and Nina Cooper. The County Juvenile Court referred Mr. and Mrs. Cooper following an incident in which Larry and some other boys were caught breaking into a neighborhood school. Some vandalism occurred, and the nurse's office was broken into. A small amount of marijuana was found on some of the boys. This is the first time Larry has gotten into trouble. A hearing has been set for June 14 to determine if Larry will be put on probation. Larry's schoolwork has been declining, and he is spending less time at home and is refusing to do household chores. Mrs. Cooper is very concerned about the possibility that her son may be involved with drugs. In an effort to prevent Larry's entry into the child welfare or juvenile justice system, the court has recommended he comply by attending your program. The purpose of the Community Youth Diversion Agency is to provide an intensive program for counseling and support to families who have children at risk. The family has requested the program's services and is willing to cooperate. However, they are also aware that the alternative to involvement in the program is to deal with the child welfare or juvenile justice system.

Larry's impending placement in the child welfare or juvenile justice system for delinquent behavior is a main concern. Larry's behavior and possible use of drugs is another concern. Mr. Cooper's job-related accident and subsequent unemployment have contributed to family breakdown and a possible alcohol dependency. Mrs. Cooper has a desire to reduce the number of hours she works in order to spend more time with her family. Jennifer needs to be able to reduce her household responsibilities, which would allow her the opportunity to develop outside interests and or activities. LaDonna is in need of a medical checkup and completion of her immunizations. Mrs. Cooper's mother, Mrs. Hayes, has a strong desire to relinquish her responsibilities as LaDonna's primary caregiver and return to her assisted-living arrangement.

Family Background

The Cooper family is a three-generation family living in a rented five-room house. The family has stable housing in a lower-middle-class neighborhood, where they have lived for ten years. Mr. and Mrs. Cooper have been married for seventeen years.

Larry Cooper, Sr.

Mr. Cooper was employed regularly as a semiskilled construction worker until he was injured in a work-related accident two years ago. He was injured by a wall that fell in on him, and he almost died before he was rescued. His back was injured and several bones were broken. He received Worker's Compensation benefits until the doctors reported six months ago that he was fit for employment. However, he states that he still has back pain and has trouble breathing at times. Presently he is doing odd jobs in the neighborhood and spending the majority of his time with his friends at a neighborhood tavern. Mr. Cooper does want to help his son; however, his work-related accident two years ago has left him with a great deal of stress. Although the doctors told him he could go back to work, the thought of going back to work results in anxiety manifested through back pain and being unable to catch his breath. Clearly, Mr. Cooper is unhappy with his unemployed status. In addition, he is burdened by the reality that he is no longer the main provider for his family and that the burden has been put on his wife. When he speaks of his desire to provide for his family by returning to work, he shows visible signs of anxiety. He admits to spending most of his time with his friends at a neighborhood tavern to escape his wife's "nagging" about his unemployment status.

Nina Cooper

Mrs. Cooper is working two jobs. She has been working on a full-time basis as a nurse's aide in a hospital for seven years. Mr. Cooper's Worker's Compensation benefits ended six months ago, and at that time she took on an additional part-time job. She became a part-time cook for ten hours a week. Her work status was supposed to be temporary, and she is getting tired of carrying the overall financial responsibility, although she enjoys the work and the friends she has made at the restaurant. Her husband is rarely home and has a bad attitude toward her and the children when he is there. The church had been a valuable support system to the Cooper family. However, she states that the family has not attended for several months.

Mrs. Cooper expressed her love for her son and said that she does not want him to enter the child welfare or juvenile justice system. However, she is disappointed, because she feels he should have known better than to become involved in such behavior. Although her relationship with her son has been a good one, she admits she has "not been there for him recently." For this reason, she blames herself for her son's predicament. Mrs. Cooper realizes that her relationship with Mr. Cooper is not as good as it used to be, and when she brings it up to him it always ends in an argument. She is hoping that despite their difficulties they can work together for the sake of their son. Mrs. Cooper is very concerned with the possibility that her son may be involved with drugs.

Jennifer

Jennifer is the oldest child of Larry, Sr., and Nina. She is in the tenth grade and presently attends Belleville East High School. She appears "out of sorts" with a flat affect. In the current situation, most of the heavy housework has become her responsibility. She is also supposed to make sure Larry does his share of the chores, but he usually does not and the two of them argue a lot about this, which results in her doing the majority of the work. She complains that she has to do everything, and she has no extra time for school activities or money for clothes. She is not a strong student and wants to quit school when she is 16, even if it means getting pregnant to do so. She has expressed an interest in being married as soon as possible to her boyfriend, Chad, who is 19. He graduated last year and works in a local garage. Jennifer longs for a normal life and feels that if she must keep house for someone she wants it to be for someone who appreciates her.

Larry, Jr.

Larry, Jr., is the second and only male child of Larry, Sr., and Nina. He is in the sixth grade. He is a friendly and verbal young man. He attends Stevenson Elementary School. Reports from the school, based on standardized tests, put him at grade level in all subjects. However, Nina has been concerned on several occasions in the last two years about Larry's report cards. His teacher currently reports that Larry is experiencing some difficulty in concentrating, has been called on frequently for minor behavior incidents, and his overall performance is continually declining. Larry has no unusual medical history. Larry and his father used to be close. They would spend a lot of time together, especially on weekends. Larry states that his dad does not feel good enough now to do some of the things they used to do together. He has expressed a desire that his father be well, so they could spend more time together and do some of the things they used to do. He states that he wishes his mother did not have to work in the evenings. Larry has been sleeping on the sofa since his grandmother came to live with them. He expresses a desire to return to his own bedroom. He has been spending more and more time after school with his friends, and is not home much these days.

Larry explained that on the night of the school incident he and his friends were just hanging out because he had nothing else to do. Larry has been friends with these boys for about three months. He states that he has not been involved before in this type of behavior: things just got out of hand. He said they got the marijuana from one of the boys' older brothers and that some had tried it, but he had not. He indicated that it really did not make any difference if he did try it, since no one really cares.

LaDonna

LaDonna is the youngest child of Larry, Sr., and Nina. She appears small for her age and rather quiet, but the family reports that she is in good health. She missed her last medical checkup and is in need of immunizations. They were never completed due to financial strain from her father's accident and subsequent unemployment. LaDonna expresses a strong attachment to her grandmother, Mrs. Hayes, with very little physical or emotional contact toward her mother.

Extended Family

Mrs. Fannie Hayes, Mrs. Cooper's mother, moved in with the family to help out after Mr. Cooper's accident and subsequent unemployment. She is a widow. Her husband passed away seven years ago from a heart attack. She used to work as a nurse's aide but is presently on disability. Due to a heart condition, high blood pressure, and varicose veins, she is unable to be on her feet for very long. She does light housekeeping and provides child care for LaDonna. Although she and LaDonna have become very close, she wishes to return to her assisted-living arrangement. She states that she was never very friendly with Mr. Cooper, but had always respected him for being a good provider. Mrs. Hayes loves her daughter yet lacks understanding as to why her daughter tolerates Mr. Cooper's unwillingness to go back to work.

Mr. and Mrs. Robert and Roberta Cooper, Mr. Cooper's parents, moved to Arizona four years ago. Robert Cooper had retired from a factory position after thirty years of service. Roberta Cooper chose to be a stay-at-home mother and homemaker. She suffers from emphysema, and her physician suggested that the climate in the west would be more conducive to her overall health. Robert and Roberta Cooper love their son, daughter-in-law, and their grandchildren very much. However, since they have relocated they are no longer able to provide the physical support they once had by taking the family out for dinners, shopping with the children, and babysitting the children daily and over entire weekends. Larry, Sr., states he grew up in a very loving and supportive home. Larry, Sr., states that his father is a reformed alcoholic; however, he had a strong work ethic, and ability to provide for his family was never an issue.

THE KANE-GRANT FAMILY (GAY TEENAGER)

Student Instructions

You are working at a public child welfare agency as a foster care case worker. You have been working with Jay Grant for about five years. Jay has just disclosed to his foster mother that he thinks he is gay. You have been instructed to assess his case and make an independent living plan for him, because the foster mother is afraid for him to stay in the home with other foster children. He has not been very cooperative with you or with any of his other case workers in the past. The state requires that your agency work with Jay until he is 19 years old.

Family Composition

This family consists of a single foster mother, Natalie Kane, age 56, and her four foster sons, Jay, age 17, Edward, age 14, Norris, age 12, and Ben, age 8. None of the boys are biological brothers.

Presenting Problem

The Department of Children and Family Services' (DCFS) social history reports indicate Jay's presenting problem as poor anger management, impulsive decision making, fear of rejection and attachment issues, and a long history of structured residential treatment facilities as a result of early abandonment by both birth parents. Jay's emotional and behavioral difficulties presented at a very young age and became more severe as he reached adolescence. Jay's mother, Shelia, abandoned her three boys to the care of their maternal grandmother when Jay was an infant. Shelia had a chronic and severe drug and alcohol problem and was unable to care for her children. Her parental rights were terminated when Jay was 6 years old. He is feeling very depressed these days because he thinks he might be gay. He has admitted it to his foster parent, and she has taken him to church so they could pray for him.

Current Situation

Jay recently was moved from residential care to a foster home placement. He was in a number of residential facilities for ten years. He resides with Ms. Kane, a single parent, and three other foster brothers. Jay has adjusted fairly well to this placement and gets along well with his foster brothers. He has learned to follow directions from his foster mother to get his needs and wants met. He does attempt to use manipulation to get his way, but he will eventually back down to "appease" his foster mother if she is adamant about a given issue. Jay has threatened to run away and go live with his girlfriend on a couple of occasions, but he has not followed through. He has a history of running away when he does not get his way.

Family Background

Jay's maternal grandmother took care of him for the first four years of his life. She passed away when he was 4; it was at this time that Jay and his brothers were placed in foster homes. Jay lived in the first home from ages 4 to 5 and his second home from 5 to 7. Both of these placements were ended due to unmanageable behaviors including severe temper tantrums, fecal smearing, aggression toward others, and property destruction.

Jay's second set of foster parents had hoped to adopt him, yet were not able to adopt him or keep others in the household safe when he threw aggressive tantrums. Jay then moved to his third foster home to be with his two other brothers, and there were plans for all three to be adopted by this family. At this time, Jay was 7 years old, labeled as a learning- and behaviorally disabled child, and attending outpatient counseling to address his problematic behaviors.

His first psychiatric hospitalization occurred when he was 8 after he hit his younger foster sister with a baseball bat. His daily problematic behaviors consisted of lying, stealing, aggression, cruelty to animals, and one known incident of sexually acting out with his foster sister. Jay needed constant supervision. He was hospitalized for two weeks and then placed at Englewood Children's Home for the next two years. During this time, Jay maintained contact with his brothers and foster family, in hopes of reuniting with them.

Jay was discharged from residential care and was able to maintain placement in his prior foster home, but not without difficulties. Jay's tantrums continued to be a concern, and his problematic behaviors consisted of severe aggression toward others and property. He was again caught sexually acting out with his foster sister, and his immediate removal from the home was demanded—this time, with no plans for a reunion.

Jay was then placed in shelter care for the next two months while waiting for a residential placement. At age 11½, he was placed in the locked unit at Angel Children's Home. Reports from this institution stated that Jay had incidents of sexually acting out with male peers, was defiant, impulsive, aggressive, manipulative, and ran away when he was transferred from the locked unit to a regular residential unit. He remained at Angel for the next two years and was then discharged due to his continued aggressive outbursts, lack of motivation to change, and limited acceptance for his actions—or in general, lack of progress in the program.

At age 14, Jay was again placed in shelter care at Hope House as he awaited an opening at the Children's Center for Behavior Disorders (CCBD). It was during this shelter care that Jay had his second psychiatric hospitalization due to impulsive risk-taking behaviors. He jumped out a second-story window in an attempt to run away, following taunts from peers about having no family. Jay remained in the hospital for two weeks, was returned to Hope House, and then placed at CCBD to receive treatment for his sexually inappropriate behaviors.

Jay spent the next three years at CCBD, and although he had no further incidents of sexually acting out, he did continue to have a problem with anger management and impulse control. He now resides with Ms. Kane, a single foster mother, and her three other foster children. He has recently admitted that he thinks he might be gay and thinks he wants to experiment with his sexual identity. His foster mother is upset over this recent admission and is afraid for the other foster children in the home, but she does not want to turn her back on Jay because he has been through so much in his life. She has told him that he should pray about those evil thoughts and the Lord will help him. He is confused because he does not feel that his thoughts are evil but he does feel that his life is confusing and that he has had a bad life. He thinks maybe he should try and live on his own, but he does not think he can make it.

Extended Family

There is no current information regarding Jay's extended family. Since parental rights were terminated several years ago, no information is available about his biological mother's whereabouts or her current substance abuse status. The identity of his biological father is unknown. He has been given the name of three possible people, any of whom could be his father. Jay's maternal grandmother died when he was 4 years old, and there has been no contact with either of Jay's older brothers in the last five years, at their request. They continue to have animosity toward him and continue to blame him for his sexually acting out with their then foster sister. Jay has been dating the same girl for quite some time. Although he is very controlling over her at times, she may be the closest thing to a family for Jay. He also does not know how to tell her that he thinks he might be gay. His girlfriend has indicated that she wants to marry him. They are very close friends and he does not want to hurt her.

THE LANDERS FAMILY (CHILD WITH UNIDENTIFIED ANGER ISSUES)

Student Instructions

You are a social worker with a private child and family agency, and the Landers family has been referred to you by their case worker with the Department of Children and Family Services (DCFS). This family has a history with DCFS, and your agency has been specifically asked to assess why Karen, age 8, is displaying violent and aggressive behaviors.

Family Composition

Karen Landers is an 8-year-old Caucasian female who is tall and overweight for her age. Karen has resided with her maternal grandmother, Ena Landers, age 57, for two years. Karen lives with her sisters, Minnie, age 10, Jessie, age 6, and brothers, Greg, age 11, and Donald, age 3.

Barbara Landers, Karen's mother, age 28, does not live in the home. Barbara Landers receives supervised visitation at the DCFS office once a week. Joseph Nicholls, Karen's biological father, age 33, does not live in the home, and his whereabouts are unknown. Charles Landers, Karen's maternal grandfather, age 57, does not live in the home, his address is unknown, and he has no contact with the family.

Current Situation

Family service is requested due to a referral from the DCFS case worker. Karen and her other siblings are receiving family counseling as part of her brother, Greg's, comprehensive treatment plan.

According to DCFS records, Karen has historically been the "good child," with very few incidents of acting out or unmanageable behavior. Since last year, however, Karen has been demonstrating severe acting out behaviors at home and in the community. She began to have frequent tantrums at her after-school program when it was time to go home. She would kick, scream, and yell during these episodes. The after-school program staff was unable to manage Karen during these episodes. Ena Landers was typically called to settle Karen down, and on occasion police intervention was required. Karen was expelled from the after-school program two months ago. She has also become increasingly defiant at home, and she is becoming more physically and verbally aggressive. Karen was recently diagnosed with posttraumatic stress disorder as a result of physical and emotional abuse she sustained, according to her pediatrician.

Ena Landers, Karen's maternal grandmother, reports that Karen has difficulty accepting the consequences of her behavior. Karen argues, cries, and attempts to fight with her grandmother whenever she receives punishment for inappropriate behavior. Karen takes things from her siblings and then lies about it. Karen's grandmother states that she and Karen have always had a conflictual relationship and their conflicts often result in physical fighting. She further states that Karen often instigates fights and arguments with her older brother and younger sister. She reports that Karen's behavior appears to be more manageable since her Ritalin dosage has been increased three weeks ago. Karen rarely is able to admit when she is wrong or is misbehaving.

Karen attends Mason Elementary School and is in the third grade. Her grades are average. Her teachers says that Karen is a very bright child who does not seem to apply herself. Karen's teacher reported that in the last two months Karen's behavior has become more problematic. Her teacher also reports that Karen has become more oppositional, and verbally and physically aggressive toward her and the other students in the class. Her teacher reports that Karen constantly complains that she does not want to go home. Because of her behavior the school is considering Karen for special education services. The teacher and other school officials believe that something is happening within the home that disturbs Karen.

Karen admits having problems respecting others' boundaries and acknowledges having difficulty accepting consequences. Karen denies knowing what upsets her when she has a tantrum at school or at home. She also denies not wanting to go home, but says she just wants to stay at school. Karen says that she likes to be at school, because her friend Darlene is there, and she likes to play with her.

Family Background Information

Karen is the third of five children born to Barbara Landers. Karen can be very pleasant and cooperative, but shows a continuous effort to displease adults. She displays an interest in reading and in art activities, and she is very creative. Karen attended Sampson Elementary School two years ago while she was in foster care. Karen's teacher at Sampson Elementary reports that Karen appeared to be well adjusted and displayed few behavioral problems. Karen's biological mother had her admitted to St. Joseph's Hospital's psychiatric unit five years ago, where Karen was diagnosed with attention deficit disorder and prescribed Ritalin.

Karen's oldest sister, Minnie, was placed in foster care in Alabama eight years ago after Barbara Landers asked for her removal, stating that Minnie had some "deep-rooted problems" and that she could no longer manage her behavior. One year later, Minnie was returned home.

DCFS records report that all of Barbara Landers's paramours have been alcoholics, drug abusers, and physically abusive toward her. Barbara was married to Raymond Bethany for two years, but they only stayed together for three months. Donald, age 3, was conceived from this relationship. During the marriage, Mr. Bethany was physically abusive toward Barbara and the children. DCFS social history reports that Mr. Bethany would lock the children in a room for days at a time with no access to food, water, or bathroom facilities.

Barbara's family has a history of violence, mental illness, and substance abuse. Barbara denies the use of drugs or alcohol, but reports she smokes cigarettes. DCFS records describe her childhood as physically and emotionally abusive. Barbara reported to DCFS that she has not seen her father, Charles Landers, since she was 5 years old. DCFS records report that Barbara Landers has a history of psychiatric treatment, which included psychotropic medications and two hospitalizations. According to DCFS reports, Barbara's mother, Ena Landers, reported to DCFS that she used to have a drinking problem ten years ago. Reports indicate that Ena Landers relinquished custody of Barbara to the state of California when she was 16 years old due to emotional problems. Other reports state that Barbara requested removal from her mother's home due to severe physical and emotional abuse.

Barbara has one younger brother, Ted, who resides near his mother. Charles Landers has served time in prison for aggravated sexual abuse. He was reportedly an accomplice to the rape of a 12-year-old girl. (Records indicate he watched the rape, but did not participate.) DCFS records report that Charles Landers also has a drug problem and attended five Narcotics Anonymous meetings while incarcerated.

Four years ago Ena and her daughter Barbara were involved in a domestic dispute that resulted in two of Barbara's children being hurt. DCFS responded, and the report substantiated physical abuse to Karen and her older sister, Minnie. Barbara Landers hit her mother in the head with a telephone, causing a head injury that required twenty-one stitches. According to DCFS records, the incident also involved pushing, shoving, and throwing ashtrays, glasses, and china, all while Barbara's children were present. The children were subsequently taken into protective custody.

Karen and her siblings were sexually abused four years ago by Barbara Landers's boyfriend, Keith Anderson. According to DCFS records, Ena Landers returned home and found Greg in the bathroom with Mr. Anderson. When she asked Greg what happened, Greg said that Mr. Anderson wanted him to "suck his pee-pee." When Barbara was informed that the children had been sexually abused, she phoned DCFS to have the children removed from her care, stating that this was the second time this had happened and she just could not go through it again. At that time, Barbara's report of neglect of the children was substantiated. Barbara also knew that Mr. Anderson was an ex-convict who had been convicted in the rape of a 10-year-old girl. After this incident, Karen and her siblings were placed in foster care. Two years later they were placed with their maternal grandmother, Ena Landers.

Extended Family

Ted Landers, Karen's uncle, age 26, lives near the family and visits his mother and the children frequently. Keith Anderson, Barbara's former boyfriend, age 35, is currently on probation and resides in a small town about twenty-five miles from Ena Landers and the children.

SAFETY AND RISK ASSESSMENT QUESTIONS

Physical Abuse

1. What form of physical abuse is present in this family?

2. What are the specific injuries to the child or children?

3. How do these injuries determine intervention?

4. How does the abuse impact protection of the child or other children in the home?

5. Does the abuse impact family preservation? Explain.

6. What cultural factors must be considered in the determination of what constitutes physical abuse in this family?

7. How do these factors impact your perception or ability to work with this family?

Neglect

8. What forms of neglect are present in this family?

9. How do these forms of neglect impact the protection of the child or children in the family?

10. How does the issue of neglect determine intervention?

11. Does the neglect impact family preservation? Explain.

12. What cultural factors must be considered in the determination of what constitutes neglect in this family?

13. How do these factors impact your perception or ability to work with this family?

14. What resources are available or accessible to the family to reduce or prevent further neglect?

15. What community factors contribute to the presenting neglect issue?

Emotional and/or Verbal Abuse

16. What form of emotional or verbal abuse is present in this family?

17. What are the specific injuries to the child or children?

18. How do these injuries determine intervention?

19. How does the abuse impact protection of the child or children in the home?

20. Does the abuse impact family preservation? Explain.

21. What cultural factors must be considered in the determination of what constitutes emotional or verbal abuse?

22. How do these factors impact your perception or ability to work with this family?

23. How does your definition or perception of emotional and/or verbal abuse contribute to your assessment?

Sexual Abuse

24. What form of sexual abuse is present in this family?

25. What are the specific injuries and type of abuse to the child or children?

26. What other forms of abuse or neglect are present in this family?

27. How does each of those forms identified manifest themselves in the family relationships?

28. How do the injuries determine intervention?

29. How does the abuse impact protection of the child or other children in the home?

30. Does the abuse impact family preservation? Explain.

31. What cultural factors must be considered in the determination of what constitutes sexual abuse in this family?

32. How do these factors impact your perception or ability to work with this family?

33. What identifiable situations or patterns contribute to the sexual abuse of the child or children (boundaries, gifts, etc.)?

34. How would your perception change if you were aware of prior abuse to the alleged perpetrator?

FAMILY CASE ANALYSIS—ENGAGEMENT

1. What is the presenting problem? How are the family members involved in the situation defining the problem?

2. In exploring the situation, how does the information that you learn from other family members inform your perceptions?

3. How would you define the working problem based on the current information?

4. What strategies do you think would be useful in engaging with the individuals involved?

FAMILY ASSESSMENT

1. How would your definition of the working problem direct your assessment?

2. What assumptions about human and social behavior are you making, and how would you follow up with these?

3. Are there other problems or issues you think might emerge as you delve deeper into this case? What are they, and how might they affect the situation?

4. What information are you lacking about the situation and its context that you feel you need to know to gain an in-depth understanding?

5. Identify the strengths, limitations, and barriers present in this family. Based on the strengths, where would you start to work with this family?

6. What issues of motivation and/or resistance do you think you are likely to encounter? How do you think you might handle them?

7. Give a clear and concise summary of your assessment, and state how it affects the defining of general goals.

8. Identify and briefly state at least two theoretical frameworks or approaches that would guide your intervention in working with this family.

9. Prepare a genogram and an ecomap for the family, using the blanks given as Figures 6.1 and 6.2.

PLANNING FOR THE FAMILY

1. State your general goals in working with this family.

2. State specific objectives related to each goal, and identify specific changes in the situation that might lead to accomplishing the above goals.

3. What actions should be taken by the worker, the clients, or others to operationalize your objectives?

4. How are you going to set up your evaluation to track accomplishments or progress in goals and objectives? (*Note:* This section should reflect knowledge of methods of practice evaluation.)

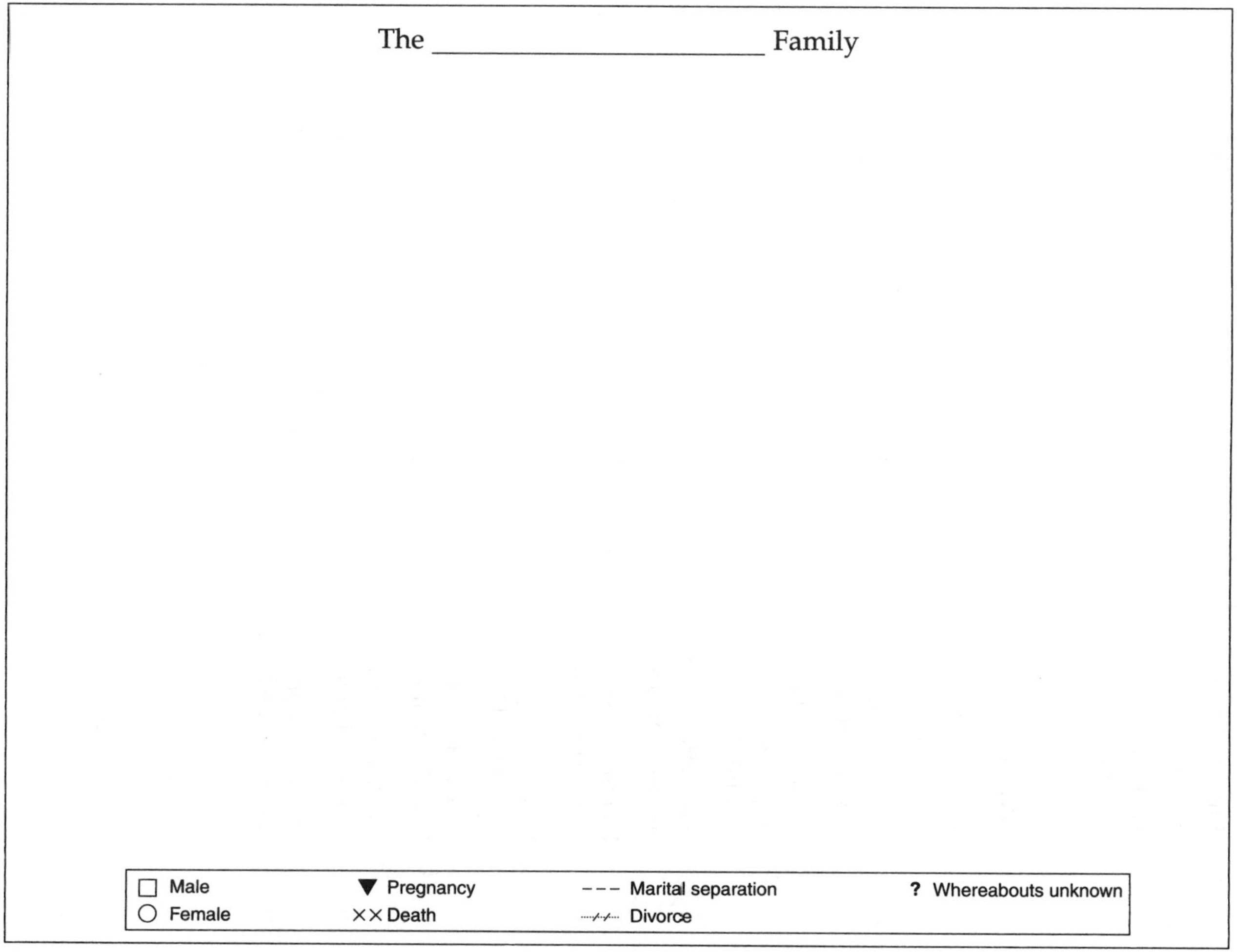

The _____ Family

Male
Female

▼ Pregnancy
✕✕ Death

– – – Marital separation
··/·/··· Divorce

? Whereabouts unknown

FIGURE 6.1   The Family Genogram
(Sketch a genogram of the facts of this family structure.)

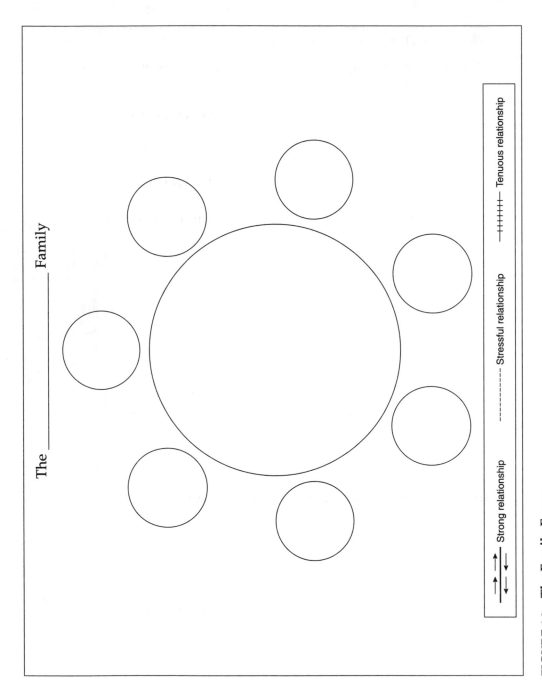

The _____ Family

Strong relationship — Stressful relationship — Tenuous relationship

FIGURE 6.2   The Family Ecomap

FAMILY TREATMENT PLAN/ CONTRACT

Design a treatment plan for this family. This is an example of a treatment/contract plan. Most practice texts provide examples.

The Brown Family Treatment/Contract Plan

Client: _____ (Define the client here.)

I. **Brief Description of the Problem**
(This is generally a summary of the reasons the client came to you or your agency.)

II. **Primary Goals and Objectives** (Find a format that is clear to your client and you.)
    1. Goal:

        Objective:

    2. Goal:

        Objective:

    3. Goal:

        Objective:

III. **We, the undersigned, agree to the following tasks:**
    1.

    2.

IV. **Evaluation of Progress** (How your plan will be evaluated.)

_____

_____   _____
                                           Signature of Social Worker

_____
Signature(s) of Client(s)

_____   _____
(Date)   (Date)

SUGGESTED READINGS

Abbott, D. A., Meredith, W. H., Self-Kelly, R., & Davis, M. E. (1997). The influence of a big brothers program on the adjustment of boys in single-parent families. *The Journal of Psychology, 131*(2), 143–156.

Akers, R. L., & Lee, G. (1999). Age, social learning, and social bonding in adolescent substance use. *Deviant Behavior, 20*(1), 1–25.

Andrews, A. B., & Asher, B. A. (1999). Measuring and monitoring children's well-being across the world. *Social Work, 44*(2), 105–115.

Astor, R. A., Behre, W. J., Wallace, J. M., & Fravil, K. A. (1998). School social workers and school violence: Personal safety, training, and violence programs. *Social Work, 43*(3), 223–232.

Balsanek, J. (1997). Addressing at-risk pregnant women's issues through community individual and corporate grassroots efforts. *Health and Social Work, 22*(1), 63–69.

Beckerman, A. (1998). Charting a course: Meeting the challenge of permanency planning for children with incarcerated mothers. *Child Welfare, 75*(5), 513–529.

Berson, N., & Meisburger, D. (1998). Working with avoidant children: A clinical challenge. *Child Welfare, 75*(4), 427–439.

Bowen, N. K. (1999). A role for school social workers in promoting student success through school-family partnerships. *Social Work in Education, 21*(1), 34–37.

Brooks, D., Barth, R. P., Bussiere, A., and Patterson, G. (1999). Adoption and race: Implementing the multiethnic placement act and the interethnic adoption provisions. *Social Work, 44*(2), 167–178.

Brown, S. R. (1996). Children, families, and HIV/AIDS: Psychosocial and therapeutic issues. *Health and Social Work, 21*(4), 312.

Carten, A. J. (1996). Mothers in recovery: Rebuilding families in the aftermath of addiction. *Social Work, 41*(2), 214–223.

Chen, Z., & Kaplan, H. B. (1997). The impact of family structure during adolescence on deviance in early childhood. *Deviant Behavior, 18*(4), 365–391.

Combs-Orme, T., & Thomas, K. H. (1997). Assessment of troubled families. *Social Work Research, 21*(4), 261–269.

Corcoran, J. (1998). Solution-focused practice with middle and high school at-risk youths. *Social Work in Education, 20*(4), 232–243.

Courney, M. E., & Barth, R. P. (1996). Pathways of older adolescents out of foster care: implications for independent living services. *Social Work, 41*(1), 75–83.

Debaryshe, B. D. (1998). A developmental perspective on anger: Family and peer contexts. *Psychology in the Schools, 35*(3), 205–227.

Dore, M. M., Nelson-Zluplo, L., & Kaufmann, E. (1999). Friends in need: Designing and implementing a psychoeducational group for school children from drug-involved families. *Social Work, 44*(2), 179–190.

Douglass, A. (1996). Rethinking the effects of homelessness on children: Resiliency and competency. *Child Welfare, 75*(6), 741–751.

Draimin, B. H., Gamble, I., Shire, A., & Hudis, J. (1998). Improving permanency planning in families with HIV disease. *Child Welfare, 77*(2), 180–194.

Duran-Aydintug, C., & Causey, K. A. (1996). Child custody determination: Implications for lesbian mothers. *Journal of Divorce and Remarriage, 25*(1/2), 55–74.

DuRant, R. H., Krowchuk, D. P., & Sinal, S. H. (1998). Victimization, use of violence, and drug use at school among male adolescents who engage in same-sex sexual behavior. *The Journal of Pediatrics, 133*(1), 113–118.

Edwards, W. J. (1996). Operating within the mainstream: Coping and adjustment among a sample of homosexual youths. *Deviant Behavior, 17*(2), 229–251.

Gardner, H. (1996). The concept of family: Perceptions of children in family foster care. *Child Welfare, 75*(2), 161–182.

Gupta, G. R. (1996). AIDS and the new orphans: Coping with death. *Journal of Comparative Family Studies, 27*(3), 582–584.

Hayes, H. D. (1997). Using integrated theory to explain the movement into juvenile delinquency. *Deviant Behavior, 18*(2), 161–184.

Hollingsworth, L. D. (1998). Promoting same-race adoption for children of color. *Social Work, 43*(2), 104–116.

Jackson, A. P. (1999). The effects of non resident father involvement on single black mothers and their children. *Social Work, 44*(2), 156–166.

Jenson, J. M., & Howard, M. O. (1998). Youth crime, public policy, and practice in the juvenile justice system: Recent trends and needed reforms. *Social Work, 43*(4), 324–334.

Johnson, N. P., & Leopard, K. L. (1996). Characteristics of children living in group homes. *Journal of Health & Social Policy, 7*(3), 35–45.

Kingery, P. M., Coggeshall, M. B., & Alford, A. A. (1998). Violence at school: Recent evidence from four national surveys. *Psychology in the Schools, 35*(3), 247–258.

Kressierer, K. D., & Bryant, C. D. (1996). Adoption as deviance: Socially constructed parent-child kinship as a stigmatized and legally burdened relationship. *Deviant Behavior, 17*(4), 391–415.

Larson, J. (1998). Managing student aggression in high schools: Implications for practice. *Psychology in the Schools, 35*(3), 283–295.

Lewis, M., Giovannoni, J. M., & Leake, B. (1997). Two-year placement outcomes of children removed at birth from drug-using and non-drug-using mothers in Los Angeles. *Social Work Research, 21*(2), 81–90.

Lichtenstein, T. (1995). To tell or not to tell: Factors affecting adoptees' telling their adoptive parents about their search. *Child Welfare, 75*(1), 61–72.

Mallon, G. P. (1998). After care, then where? Outcomes of an independent living program. *Child Welfare, 77*(1), 61–78.

Morrison, M., & Doris, J. M. (1998). Preventing child placement in substance-abusing families: Research-informed practice. *Child Welfare, 77*(4), 407–426.

Otta, E. (1997). Assigning a name to a child: Gender differences in two over lapping generations. *The Journal of Psychology, 131*(2), 133–142.

Richman, J. M., Rosenfeld, L. B., & Bowen, G. L. (1998). Social support for adolescents at risk of school failure. *Social Work, 43*(4), 309–323.

PRACTICE LAB: SKILLS AND GRADING CRITERIA

SKILL	DESCRIPTION	RATING (4 IS HIGHEST)	COMMENTS (THINGS THAT WORKED WELL; SUGGESTIONS FOR IMPROVEMENT; "PLUSES AND WISHES")
Avoiding barriers	Social worker refrains from lecturing, moralizing, judgmentality, or otherwise "talking down" to client.	4 3 2 1	
Professional use of self	Social worker shows awareness of client needs and preferences overall; shows self-awareness and appropriate self-disclosure and boundary setting.	4 3 2 1	
Diversity	Social worker shows awareness of and sensitivity to diversity variables such as race/ethnicity; religion; age; gender; sexual orientation; (dis)ability status.	4 3 2 1	

(continued)

SKILL	DESCRIPTION	RATING (4 IS HIGHEST)	COMMENTS (THINGS THAT WORKED WELL; SUGGESTIONS FOR IMPROVEMENT; "PLUSES AND WISHES")
Empathy	Social worker consistently demonstrates empathic responding at Level 2 or better (involves a clear and accurate response to both feelings and situation).	4 3 2 1	
Problem identification	Social worker identifies, in collaboration with client, a clear, concrete, and specific working problem from a range of concerns presented by client.	4 3 2 1	
Assessment	Social worker explores (at a minimum) harm risk, social support, coping strategies, and strengths of the client system and significant others, including the social environment.	4 3 2 1	
Planning and goal setting	Social worker, in collaboration with client, identifies options for problem resolution, including pros and cons of the options. Goals are identified with client, and are clear, concrete, and "doable."	4 3 2 1	

SKILL	DESCRIPTION	RATING (4 IS HIGHEST)	COMMENTS (THINGS THAT WORKED WELL; SUGGESTIONS FOR IMPROVEMENT; "PLUSES AND WISHES")
Intervention	Social worker identifies, with client, an intervention plan, including a clear description of roles and activities for both client and social worker.	4 3 2 1	
Evaluation	Social worker identifies, with client, a mechanism for monitoring progress and evaluating how the intervention plan is working.	4 3 2 1	
Termination	Social worker discusses with the client at case closure a review and plan for follow-up.	4 3 2 1	

Overall, I give this interview the following rating (circle one):   4   3   2   1

Main strength of this interview/this social worker:

Main area needing work:

Source: Kathleen Tunney, Southern Illinois University, Edwardsville, IL. Printed with permission.

INDEX